Over the past decade, I have wa[...] on his knees and seek the heart [...] circumstances. The honesty and [...] his process has allowed him to become a trusted voice in my life—and through this book, I believe he can become the same to you.

KYLE KORVER, NBA veteran

Jarrett Stevens is a dear friend and a deep soul. And what he has given us through this book is a real gift. If you're looking to connect with God in real and authentic ways but find yourself stuck or lost, this book is for you. Through refreshing honesty and humor and spiritually practical wisdom, *Praying Through* helps you find your way to deeper places with God no matter what season you find yourself in.

MIKE FOSTER, founder of People of the Second Chance, host of *Fun Therapy* podcast

There are many books out there on prayer, but not like this one. *Praying Through* is not just theoretical or overly mystical or written so long ago that it is hard to apply today. It doesn't leave you feeling defeated and guilty because you aren't praying enough. It is an encouraging, practical, real-life, sticking-to-the-actual-Bible-teachings guide to prayer. By the end of this book, because it relates to the real struggles we have today, you will find yourself becoming increasingly aware of how much God loves us, and you'll pray more naturally and often as a result.

DAN KIMBALL, Vintage Faith Church

I've known Jarrett for almost twenty years, and he is honestly one of the most gifted teachers around. He has a brilliant way of bringing lofty theological ideas into the messy reality of everyday life. This book is no exception. Jarrett has taken a topic that feels both overfamiliar and overwhelming and offers tangible handles and on-ramps. Through stories, Scripture, a great sense of humor, and the weighty wisdom of someone who has walked the journey for many years, this book will help you move from feeling paralyzed by the idea of prayer to saying, "I can do this!"

AARON NIEQUIST, author of *The Eternal Current*

We serve a conversational God, a God who wants to know us and who wants us to know him through every season of life. What Jarrett has done through this book is to uncomplicate what so many Christians have complicated: how to simply have a conversation with God. I thank God for this book and for my friend Jarrett.

CARLOS WHITTAKER, author of *Kill the Spider* and *Moment Maker,* host of *Enter Wild* podcast

You don't find many books on prayer that are written in the voice of this generation. This is that kind of book! *Praying Through* is honest, hilarious, and helpful. Jarrett has a way of turning deep spiritual disciplines into helpful habits that we can actually practice in each and every season of life. No matter where you're at with God or with prayer, this book is for you!

SAM COLLIER, host of *A Greater Story* podcast, speaker and host at North Point Ministries

As the daughter of a pastor, I grew up around prayer. It was like a second language in our home. But just because I grew up *around* prayer doesn't mean that I grew up *in* prayer. Over the years, I've found myself occasionally stuck and lost, passionless and purposeless in prayer. We all have. That's why I *love* this book: Jarrett Stevens has given us a deep and simple guidebook for navigating all of life's seasons through prayer. If you want to grow in prayer and your relationship with God, then TREAT YO SELF to this book!

BIANCA JUÁREZ OLTHOFF, copastor of The Father's House OC, author of *How to Have Your Life Not Suck* and *Play with Fire*

PRAYING

THROUGH

OVERCOMING THE OBSTACLES
THAT KEEP US FROM GOD

JARRETT STEVENS

A NavPress resource published in alliance
with Tyndale House Publishers

NavPress

NavPress is the publishing ministry of The Navigators, an international Christian organization and leader in personal spiritual development. NavPress is committed to helping people grow spiritually and enjoy lives of meaning and hope through personal and group resources that are biblically rooted, culturally relevant, and highly practical.

For more information, visit www.NavPress.com.

Praying Through: Overcoming the Obstacles That Keep Us from God

Copyright © 2020 by Jarrett Stevens. All rights reserved.

A NavPress resource published in alliance with Tyndale House Publishers.

NAVPRESS and the NAVPRESS logo are registered trademarks of NavPress, The Navigators, Colorado Springs, CO. Absence of ® in connection with marks of NavPress or other parties does not indicate an absence of registration of those marks.

The Team: Don Pape, Publisher; David Zimmerman, Acquisitions Editor; Elizabeth Schroll, Copy Editor; Jennifer Phelps, Designer

Author photo taken by Marcin Cymmer, copyright © 2018. All rights reserved. Cover illustration by Jen Phelps, copyright © Tyndale House Publishers. All rights reserved.

Jarrett Stevens is represented by Angela Scheff of The Christopher Ferebee Agency, www.christopherferebee.com.

For information about special discounts for bulk purchases, please contact Tyndale House Publishers at csresponse@tyndale.com, or call 1-800-323-9400.

Library of Congress Cataloging-in-Publication Data

Names: Stevens, Jarrett, author.
Title: Praying through : overcoming the obstacles that keep us from God / Jarrett Stevens.
Description: Colorado Springs : NavPress, 2020. | Includes bibliographical references.
Identifiers: LCCN 2019030307 (print) | LCCN 2019030308 (ebook) | ISBN 9781631469817 (paperback) | ISBN 9781631469824 (ebook other) | ISBN 9781631469831 (epub) | ISBN 9781631469848 (kindle edition)
Subjects: LCSH: Prayer—Christianity.
Classification: LCC BV210.3 .S774 2020 (print) | LCC BV210.3 (ebook) | DDC 248.3/2—dc23
LC record available at https://lccn.loc.gov/2019030307
LC ebook record available at https://lccn.loc.gov/2019030308

Printed in the United States of America

26	25	24	23	22	21	20
7	6	5	4	3	2	1

I dedicate this book to the lives and memories
of my father-in-law, Bill Pieczynski,
and my brother-in-law, Andy Pieczynski.

Bill (aka "Pops"),

You never allowed me to see you as a father-in-law—only as a father. Thank you for the example you gave me. For teaching me how to love your daughter well. For showing me how to change the oil in my car. For helping Jeanne and me build our first home together. For listening to early-90s hip-hop with me. For leaving me big shoes to fill.

Although you left us too soon, you left us with so many loving memories and stories. And you left me a legacy that I am still doing my best to live into.

Andy (aka "The Bison"),

My heart is still reeling and grieving and grappling with your life ending so unexpectedly and so soon.

Andy, you were a good son. A good brother. A good friend. A good uncle. And a great husband to Anto and father to Ewan. Thank you for welcoming me into your family so many years ago. Thank you for your incredible and impeccable example of faithfulness and loyalty. Thank you for loving Anto like you did. And thank you for bringing Ewan into this world. I see you in him every time I am with him. Anto and Ewan are part of our family now. They are well loved and will always be taken care of.

I miss you, brother.

And I'll see you soon.

CONTENTS

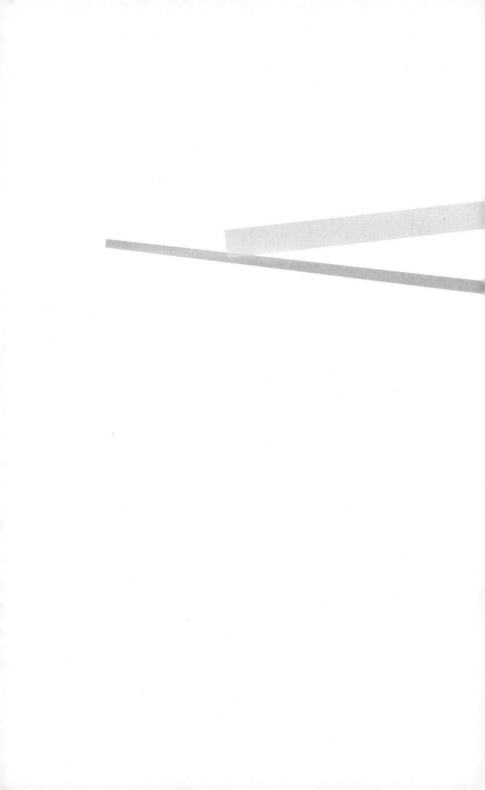

FOREWORD

To be human is to pray, although almost everybody I know feels a little uncertain about it. Christians often feel guilty about praying too little. Atheists—a surprising number of whom pray—feel guilty about praying at all.

But we're often unclear about how prayer works. One of the most famous passes in football is called a "Hail Mary." When time is running out and the end zone is a long way away, the quarterback will heave the ball into the air and—since human competence is not enough to ensure success— heave a prayer along with the ball. We say things like "You haven't got a prayer," meaning "You haven't got a *chance.*"

And yet, we pray—when we're sick, when we're scared, when we're hopeful, when we're hopeless. There is Something or Someone out there that we can't stop calling on.

Which is why Jarrett Stevens has written a guide for all kinds of prayer for all kinds of people. Jarrett reminds us that when the disciples asked Jesus to "teach us to pray,"[1] it meant that prayer is a spiritual skill that can be learned and that we never stop learning. Thomas Merton wrote about what Jarrett reminds us: When it comes to prayer, "we will never be anything else but beginners, all our life!"[2]

Part of what is so helpful about this book is how very concrete and practical it is. Prayer, in one sense, is not mysterious; it is simply taking the expressions that flow naturally and powerfully from the human condition and turning them Godward. We cheer and celebrate—which is very close to worship. We are crushed and remorseful—which is just a hair away from confession. We are desperate—and desperation lives right next door to intercession. It may be that you know more about prayer than you know. It may be that you pray more than you know.

We begin the adventure of prayer with the master prayer of all time, as Jarrett unpacks the depth of the Lord's Prayer. But the beauty of prayer is that it's as simple as single words: *Wow. Please. Help. Thanks. Yes!* The early church fathers and mothers used to say that the Gospels are so wide that anyone can learn from them, yet so deep that no one can ever plumb them. So it is with prayer. It is the great laboratory of the spirit. The most prodigal skeptic on earth can plunge in. The greatest saint on the planet has only skimmed the surface.

For prayer is as deep as God.

This book will also change the way you live and pray, because in it, Jarrett reminds us that our living *is* a form of praying. It is impossible to ask for forgiveness, for example, without living in the slipstream of forgiveness offered to others—what Dallas Willard used to call the "unity of spiritual orientation."[3]

But what is especially wonderful about Jarrett's journey is the heart of prayer, because it is in the depths of prayer—our confusion, our inadequacy, our hurt, our wonder—that we meet the depth of God. And we find there a Father more filled with love than we could imagine.

So whatever you're facing—you've picked up the right book.

You have hope.

You have a prayer.

John Ortberg

INTRODUCTION

DEAR GOD...

Prayer is not about changing God . . .
but being willing to let God change us.

RICHARD ROHR

I was almost thirty years old before I sent my first text message. It was on my Motorola flip phone, a marvel of modern technology that is now considered a relic. My friend Oomen sent me my first text: "what up, man. we should hang! :)" As profound as his text was, I had no idea *what* it was. I knew who it was from, but I didn't know how to respond. So I called him.

"Dude. What was that?"

"What was what?" he replied.

"That . . . email . . . you sent to my phone. What was that?" (Don't judge. This was the early aughts. Pre-iPhone. Pre-DM. Pre-GIF. It was a simpler time in those days.)

He told me about texting and how I could reply by

pressing the numbers on my phone multiple times to get the letters that I needed to spell the words that I wanted. (Note to millennial readers: Back then mobile phones used to serve only for making phone calls and playing the occasional game of Snake. There was no keyboard. Each number on the phone's keypad had letters associated with it: 2 = ABC, 3 = DEF, 4 = GHI, and so on. To get to the letter "C," you had to press the "2" button three times. The letter "E" took two pushes of the "3" button. You get the idea . . .) I spent the next five minutes after our call composing my first text: "thnx man. this is cool."

Fast-forward a little more than a decade. Our daughter, Gigi, was sending me texts *filled* with emojis—all the emojis—at six years old. At a very young age, our kids learned how to text. Now they send texts to their friends. They send GIFs to me and my wife. They send videos to their grandparents. To them, texting is native. They took to it naturally. What was new to me is normal to them. It's just another way they communicate.

The same could be said of prayer. It may seem new, unfamiliar, and a little clunky . . . until it isn't. Eventually prayer becomes innate and normal. Talking with God can become as natural as talking with a friend. With presence, patience, and practice, prayer becomes another way to communicate—perhaps the most important way, one that communicates the most important things about your life. It can become easier and more essential. You can and will find your way, find your voice, and—ultimately—find God more present and available than you could have ever possibly imagined.

WHEN PRAYING SEEMS HARD

I've been a pastor for more than twenty years, and I can't tell you how many times I've heard the following:

"I just don't know how to pray."
"I didn't grow up doing this kind of stuff."
"I've found it hard to pray after this loss."
"I'm too angry at God to pray right now."

I get it. I've had my fair share of frustration and struggle with prayer. Years ago, my father-in-law died suddenly and unexpectedly while running a race with his son. None of us saw it coming, and none of us saw how we would make it without him. Many months passed before I felt like talking to God again. When my workload is particularly intense (precisely the time I need to be praying the most), I tell myself the last thing I have time for is prayer. Like when my family is running late in the morning. Or when I'm exhausted at the end of the day.

I get it. Praying seems hard.

For many people, learning to pray feels like learning a second language: You're never quite sure if you're using the right words the right way. You can feel like a tourist lost in a foreign land, where everyone else knows something that you don't.

Or maybe prayer seems hard because you feel like you're

not praying enough. Ask anyone who prays how often they pray, and they will most likely tell you, in somewhat deflated and potentially shame-laden tones, "Not enough. I should be praying more." *Should* is one of the unhealthiest, most unhelpful words in the English language. It's filled with guilt and obligation, especially when it comes to prayer. Like sleeping, flossing, exercising, and eating healthily, praying is another thing that we know is good for us but just don't do *enough* of—as if there were a prayer quota that we never quite seem to reach.

Then there are times when prayer becomes hard because you just don't want to do it. You're either too tired or too busy. Or you don't feel like bothering God with your silly little prayers. Over time, praying can seem rote and repetitive, stagnant and stale. You may sense that you've run out of words to say.

And for some people, a great loss, the presence of pain, or an unwelcome season of grief makes praying feel like stumbling and fumbling around in the dark. Maybe you've experienced the flame of prayer that once burned bright but has now dwindled to a flicker at best, and you just can't see a way through the darkness.

Maybe you've found that the sweet and simple prayers of childhood faith are no longer big enough for the complexities of adult life. Formulas for prayer fall short and eventually fail us. Sometimes all the words in the world cannot seem to connect the dots from our hearts to God's. Martyn Lloyd-Jones, a famous twentieth-century Welsh minister, acknowledged the perplexity of prayer by calling it "the supreme expression of our faith in God"[1] and saying that "everything we do in the Christian life is easier than prayer."[2]

Praying is hard. Or at least that's what we tell ourselves. The goal of this book is to help you see that while prayer is mysterious, it is not as hard as you think. In fact, without being in any way even slightly patronizing, praying is honestly quite simple.

The problem for many of us is that we have forgotten how simple prayer really is: so simple that a child can do it. It's just talking with God. That's it. If you can talk to a friend, you can pray. God didn't make prayer hard—we did.

> Anyone who has committed in their heart to pray has found it hard to pray.

My kids have been praying since they could talk. Not because my wife and I are amazing parents, but because to them it's simple. They just talk to God. They pray without pretense. They use their own words to let God know how they are feeling and what they want. They pray for their friends, they pray for their schoolwork, they pray for each other. They even pray for their stuffed animals. Chiggers the Lion and Roary the Bear have been covered in prayer.

The power of prayer is in its simplicity. And yet so often we find ourselves feeling the same way Jesus' disciples did when they asked, "Lord, teach us [how] to pray" (Luke 11:1).

And if you can posture yourself like those first followers of Jesus and ask God to make prayer your way of life, I believe this book will be not only helpful but also liberating and life-giving to you. Because we need prayer more than we know.

PRAYING IS ESSENTIAL

Whether you think prayer is hard or easy or something in-between, one thing is for certain—prayer is essential. It is our lifeline. It centers us, sustains us, and connects us to a God who is for us; a God who makes himself available to us, if we just pray. Prayer is not only our way *to* God but also our way *through* life. It is our way through this beautiful and broken world. Prayer is not merely a thing we do in life but also the very *way* we do life. It is how we choose to live with God in this world. If you are going to make prayer a way of life, you must be honest about where you're at and how you feel about prayer.

Prayer is not merely a thing we do in life but also the very *way* we do life.

Not that long ago, I found myself saying good-bye to my dear friend Jeremiah, a worship leader in our church. I did not want to say good-bye. I was not prepared to say good-bye. He and his beautiful wife, Tamara, and their amazing son, Kanon, had been part of Soul City Church since the beginning. Jeremiah's death came quicker than any of us were ready for. After a year of battling lymphoma and awaiting stem cell surgery, Jeremiah left this world and went on to lead worship in the very presence of God. Jeremiah modeled for our church what it means to worship God "in the Spirit and in truth" (John 4:24). He built our prayer ministry from the overflow of his own prayer life. And as we stood there saying good-bye to a soul who was already gone, I knew I wouldn't be able to get through that season without prayer. My struggle to pray in the season following my father-in-law's death had already taught me how much I needed prayer in such times. Without a connection to God, I would be consumed by grief. I needed a safe and sacred place to cry, to grieve, to pour out my heart to a heart that is familiar with grief and loss.

Our pains and pitfalls, hurts and hungers, dramas and decisions, sadnesses and sicknesses are often our greatest paths to prayer. Sometimes it takes getting to the end of yourself for your prayer life to begin. When every door seems to have closed, *then* we are open to prayer. This isn't just true of those who are in a relationship with God. When life gets hard or out of control, even people who don't believe in God believe in prayer. Somehow we simultaneously know and forget how essential prayer is for this life. Life is too full and too fragile to *not* be supported by prayer.

Wherever you're at and whatever you're facing as you read these words, my hope—my prayer—is that you will discover prayer as your way of making it through.

YOU'RE ALREADY AWESOME

Here's the thing—you already know how to pray. It's true! No matter how hard or challenging it may seem, no matter how new you are to it or how long you've been at it, you are already awesome at praying.

> If you've ever cheered for your favorite team, you already know how to *worship*.
> If you've ever said, "I'm sorry," you already know how to *confess*.
> If you've ever worried about anything, you already know how to *meditate*.
> If you've ever talked for hours with a friend, you already know how to *talk with God*.

Simply put, prayer is all about taking the things you do naturally and making them supernatural. That doesn't mean that you won't get stuck. All of us get stuck in prayer. All of us need help. The goal of this book is to give you a way to pray through this life by offering honest reflection, biblical connections, and real-world application. You get to learn from those who've gone before you, who've faced the same struggles you have, so you can go further in your faith. The goal is not to make you a black belt in prayer but simply to help you know and fall more in love with God, to live your life so connected

Prayer is all about taking the things you do naturally and making them supernatural.

to him that you can face whatever comes your way. This is not a "Three Simple Steps" kind of book. Prayer just doesn't work that way. This book is about you accessing the power and presence of God in your everyday life. It's about you growing closer to God and becoming more of who he created you to be.

Whether you're new to prayer or have been at it a long time, my hope is that before you know it, you'll be connecting with God in deep and meaningful ways. That prayer becomes your way through this life; that it becomes as natural and normal as texting a friend. And that no matter what season you find yourself in, there is always a way to pray through.

"TAFN. THX. BRB."

1

WHEN EVERYTHING IS NEW

To pray means to be willing to be naive.

EMILIE GRIFFIN

I've torn my ACL . . . twice. The same knee. Four years apart, almost to the day. The first time was shortly after I turned forty. I had made a list of forty things that I wanted to accomplish in my fortieth year. One of them was picking up where I had left off with skateboarding some ten years prior. My resurrected skateboarding career lasted all of forty-five minutes. It ended with me clawing and crawling my way out of a six-foot-deep bowl at a skate park in Des Moines, Iowa, and driving five hours back home to Chicago . . . with a torn ACL and three Advil in my system.

The second time I tore my ACL was in the heat of battle. Our staff had converted the church into a Nerf-gun battle zone, and it was men versus women. The women, led by my wife, Jeanne, were cheating terribly. Something had to be done. Someone had to put an end to their tyranny. That someone was me . . . until, running around a corner, I heard the familiar "pop" of my left knee. I knew exactly what I had done. I had torn my ACL—playing with Nerfs.

Leading up to and well after surgery each time, I had an unpaid part-time job: going to physical therapy. Three times a week for four months, I showed up. Each time, I spent an hour to an hour and a half doing the smallest and seemingly most insignificant exercises: Balancing on one foot. Balancing on one foot while standing on a foam pad. Balancing on one foot while standing on a foam pad while throwing a ball against a wall. Walking. Stepping on and off a six-inch wooden block. Sitting. Rainy-day recess involved more exercise than this, and yet I had to do it to get back to where I had been. I had to do things that felt simple and small over and over until they became normal.

This is how prayer can seem when everything is new. It can feel slow and small and frustrating. It can feel intimidating and overwhelming. It can feel like learning to walk all over again. Or more specifically, learning to talk all over again. It can feel clumsy and repetitive and leave you wondering if you'll ever figure it out. If you're new to prayer or coming back to prayer and find yourself having this kind of reaction or experience, here's some good news—you're never going to figure it out. Encouraging, right? Here's why it's good news: You're not supposed to figure it out.

Prayer is a spiritual practice that takes . . . wait for it . . . practice. The point of prayer is not perfection but participation. No one ever figures out prayer. Now, I know what you're thinking—*But what about Jesus? He seemed to have prayer figured out.* True. Jesus is a safe answer to most spiritual questions. But even all of Jesus' prayer bona fides didn't cause him to pray any less. If anything, he prayed more. We find Jesus praying all the time. Jesus, who was fully God and fully human, chose to practice prayer, which is a great reminder

The point of prayer is not perfection but participation.

to those who have been praying for a long time. I have been praying for almost forty years, and there have been several times in my life when I needed to start over with prayer to get back to that first-crush rush that comes from connecting with God. Maybe what you most need is a do-over with prayer, and you're ready to begin again.

If you want to grow and are willing to start where you're at, you can learn to pray just like Jesus. If you're willing to ask God for help with prayer (as one of Jesus' disciples does in Luke 11:1), you are already further along than you realize. And over time, as you commit yourself to prayer, what is new right now will become a natural and necessary part of your life—something that you love to do and don't even have to think about. Just like learning to walk all over again.

EVERYTHING YOU KNOW WAS NEW ONCE

Except for a handful of things, *everything* you do you had to *learn* to do. Things like breathing and sleeping and blinking were included in the box. Everything else you had to learn.

> You learned how to eat solid foods (as well as which foods you liked and which ones you didn't like).
> You had to learn how to walk.
> You had to learn how to talk.
> You had to learn how to dress yourself (post-onesies).
> You had to learn how to read by yourself and write without autocorrect.
> You had to learn how to ride a bike.
> You had to learn math, history, and science—and how to play "Hot Cross Buns" on the recorder.
> You had to learn (albeit awkwardly) how to kiss.

I could go on and on. Just about everything you know how to do was new at some point. Either someone taught you or you figured it out on your own. No one argues that. The place where we often have a problem, however, is in admitting that we don't know things. No one likes to admit they are a newbie. Acknowledging that you don't know how to do something requires a level of humility and vulnerability that doesn't always come naturally.

During college, I landed a high-profile job in the domestic-foods export industry. Okay, I was a pizza delivery guy (but you must admit, it sounds better the other way).

One night when my car broke down, I had to borrow a coworker's car to keep making deliveries. He threw me the keys as he asked, "You know how to drive a stick (manual transmission), right?"

"Of course!" I answered. I did not. It was one of the longest nights of my life as I revved and rolled my way backward through the hills of San Francisco's East Bay. True story: It took me forty-five minutes to deliver one particular order . . . only two miles away.

Why didn't I just answer honestly? Why was it so hard to admit that I didn't know how to drive a stick shift? One word: *pride*. I didn't want my coworker to know that I didn't know. You may not think of yourself as a prideful person, but if you've ever found it hard to admit that you don't know something or have resisted being taught something new, then you have wrestled with pride. And when it comes to prayer, nothing gets in the way more than pride. Our fear of vulnerability and aversion to authenticity can keep us from intimacy with God. Pride prevents prayer. If you are not ready to admit that you don't know, then you are not ready to really grow. This is why Andrew Murray, a nineteenth-century writer and pastor, wrote that "pride must die in you or nothing of heaven can live in you."[1]

Pride prevents prayer.

If, however, you are willing to admit to God and yourself where you are *actually* at with prayer, endless possibilities await. If you can summon the courage of humility to say that you need help, you are already well on your way to an ever-expanding prayer life.

A friend recently and quite radically said yes to Jesus for the first time. As someone who had been very successful in his career and had achieved more than he ever could have dreamed, he found himself, in his midforties, starting from the beginning with God. He didn't own a Bible. He had never really prayed before. And he had never visited church more than two weeks in a row.

Beginning a relationship with God halfway through your life can be very humbling. But rather than playing into pride, he has unapologetically owned where he is at. We got him his first Bible (rather, he stole it from church, but we let that slide). He asked where he should begin in the Bible. We told him the Gospel of Mark. He finished it in a week and decided to read Matthew, Luke, and John on his own. He admitted that he had never really prayed before but wanted to learn.

At dinner recently, we talked about prayer, and he told me, "I've been praying to God, and I haven't really heard anything from him lately . . . so I've moved on to the Holy Spirit." I love it! His hunger for spiritual growth is awe-inspiring. And what is most impressive to me is his humility. When you are willing to admit where you're at, you can go just about anywhere.

Perhaps the most powerful prayer for someone who is new to prayer or coming back to it is simply this: "God, teach me how to pray." Rather than pretending you know it all or shaming yourself for not, can you muster the courage to meet Jesus where you are at and echo the simple request of one of Jesus' own disciples? To admit that you are new and to start there?

PRACTICING PRAYER

Again, think about all the things you've learned how to do up to this point in your life. My hunch is that in the process of learning whatever it is that you don't even think twice about anymore, you never stopped to think about why you didn't know how to do it. You probably didn't get all that discouraged or defeated. You just came across something that you didn't know how to do, and you tried it. And you tried it again. You might have fumbled around for a bit until you figured it out. Or you found someone else who knew how to do it, and you asked for help. But you kept doing it and kept doing it until it became second nature to you.

So it is with prayer.

Like just about everything else in your life, you start where you're at, and you try. And you try again. And you fumble around for a while. And eventually you muster enough courage to ask for help—which, in so many ways, is what you have already done by placing this book in your hands.

It all comes down to whether you are willing to learn. Are you willing to start where you're at? And are you willing to believe that God isn't waiting for you to get it all right . . . but in fact is already with you, teaching you how to pray?

TEACH ME TO PRAY

If there were a Greatest Hits of Prayer, without a doubt the Lord's Prayer (Matthew 6:9-13 and Luke 11:2-4) would top the list. It's the "Bohemian Rhapsody" of prayer . . . only with less falsetto. It's easily the most well-known prayer from the Bible, recognized around the world. This prayer has been studied, memorized, recited, and sung for some two thousand years. It is familiar to both children and adults. In the church that I grew up in, we sang it as a song on Sunday mornings. I always loved that because it built and built until the end, when everyone sang at the top of their lungs and from the bottom of their hearts, "For thine is the kiiiingdom, and the powwwwer, and the glooooorrrry foreveeeeeevvvverrrrr. Aaaaamen." It was definitely a showstopper!

But this iconic prayer that Jesus taught us did not come from some three-point sermon or prepared remarks. It came from a deep place. It came from raw and real desire. It came from Jesus recognizing that his friends, who were new to prayer—or at the very least, prayer like this—needed help. They were willing to admit that they needed help. In fact, it says in Luke 11:1,

> One day Jesus was praying in a certain place. When
> he finished, one of his disciples said to him, "Lord,
> teach us to pray, just as John taught his disciples."

What we see here is that the disciples had seen something—two somethings, to be precise:

1. They had seen Jesus pray.
2. They had seen John's disciples pray.

And they wanted what others seemed to have.

Watching Jesus Pray

At this point, the disciples had been with Jesus for a year, maybe more. They had seen Jesus pray a good bit. They noticed that he regularly pulled away from the din and demand of the crowds to seek silence and solitude. They had also heard him pray. In Luke 9, we read several accounts of Jesus praying. He prayed as he gave thanks for the miraculous provision of God at the feeding of the five thousand (verse 16). He prayed with a handful of his disciples right before his transfiguration (verses 28-29).

After seventy-two of his followers returned from their first ministry adventure, Jesus prayed while "full of joy through the Holy Spirit" (Luke 10:21). And in Luke 11:1, we see that the disciples had been watching Jesus while he prayed. They had seen Jesus pray. They had seen God the Son speak with God the Father. Jesus, the one we pray to, was a participant in prayer. This is worth considering for a moment.

Can you imagine what that would have been like? God the Son . . . praying through God the Spirit . . . to God the Father. I'm not sure if there is any purer, more potent prayer than that. And the disciples got to witness it! They got to experience it with him. It would be like sharing a driveway basketball hoop with LeBron James. Or like having Danica Patrick as your Uber driver. They had proximity to prayer in its most powerful and personal state. You'd think that watching Jesus pray would have been enough of an education for these first followers. But it wasn't. They had their eyes elsewhere as well.

Watching Others Pray

Luke 11:1 tells us that a large part of the motivation for the disciples' interest in prayer was rooted in some level of comparison and competition. They had seen the way John's disciples prayed. The John they are referring to here is Jesus' cousin, John the Baptizer. Like Jesus, he had disciples. And apparently, John had taught *his* disciples to pray. Whether out of inspiration, comparison, or competition, Jesus' disciples wanted what John's disciples seemed to have when it came to prayer. This is common for folks who are new to prayer or are coming back to it: We want what others seem to have.

I remember hearing one of my favorite authors, Anne Lamott, pray at an intimate event where she was speaking years ago. I had been praying for most of my life, but I had never prayed like she prayed. It was honest and unpolished. Raw and real. She may have even sworn in that prayer; I can't recall. But it wouldn't surprise me. This was *not* how I was taught to pray, but I was immediately captured by it. I wanted to pray like Anne Lamott prayed.

The disciples' desire and demand for Jesus to teach them to pray is an invitation for us to ask the same. The disciples were not new to prayer. As good Jewish kids, they had grown up reciting prayers and attending prayer services. Some examples of these follow:

- *the shema*—a morning and evening prayer declaring God's wholeness, holiness, and oneness
- *the shaharith*—a morning prayer service filled with blessing and naming the day's needs
- *the minhah*—an afternoon prayer service for confession and contrition
- *the maarib*—an evening prayer service for recommitting the body to God's service
- *the birkat hamazon*—a prayer of grace said after meals

These were prayers they were taught and had memorized and practiced since they were kids. They knew how to pray *these* kinds of prayers, but there was something about the way Jesus prayed that felt new. It was personal rather than polished—more in the moment rather than merely memorized. Not that there was anything wrong with the way they had been taught to pray . . . it just seemed as though there could be more. Rather than feeling intimidated, they became intrigued. So they asked Jesus for help. And help, he did.

A WAY TO PRAY

Jesus gave us a *way* to pray. Forgoing formulas and trite prayers to recite, Jesus laid out the spirit and flow of how we can come to God with all of who we are to experience all of who he is. If you're new to prayer—or like Jesus' disciples, new to this way of praying—the Lord's Prayer can be not only helpful but also transformational. Rather than rushing through it or just reciting it, let's go slowly through Matthew 6, taking a moment to find all that God has for us in this way to pray.

"Our Father in Heaven, Hallowed Be Your Name"

Right off the bat, Jesus acknowledges who God is, where he's at, and how we come to him. From this most familiar prayer, it is perhaps these first two words that we have become most familiar with: *Our Father.* They're why some folks call this prayer "the Our Father." It's not a very original title, but it is effective. In our formality and familiarity with this prayer, though, it's easy to miss what Jesus was teaching us. Many biblical scholars believe that the Aramaic word Jesus used for *Father* here is *abba. Abba* does not translate to the formality of the word *father* as we understand it but is best understood in our language as *daddy.* It's intimate. It's personal. It immediately implies the type of relationship we are meant to have with God. He is our Abba Daddy.

But this is no ordinary daddy; this is a perfect parent who is enthroned in heaven. Jesus uses the word translated as *hallowed* to deepen our relationship with God. *Hallowed* is a "Bible-y" word if ever there was one. It's not one we tend to use every day. When was the last time you described a movie as "hallowed"? Probably not recently (or often). Simply put, *hallowed* means holy, sacred, and set apart. In other words, God is our Holy Daddy who is worthy of all worship in heaven and earth . . . and yet is intimately available to us whenever we call. He's bigger than we can conceive and closer than we can imagine.

"Your Kingdom Come, Your Will Be Done, on Earth as It Is in Heaven"

Jesus continues, teaching us that we are to ask and expect God's Kingdom, will, and way to be present in our lives. This is not merely some future hope or expectation but a present manifestation in *me*. In *us*. In my home. In my neighborhood. At my work. The idea is that you and I bring God's perfect way to the often-imperfect ways of this world, that this physical realm becomes the place where we practice what is commonplace in heaven.

"Give Us Today Our Daily Bread"

Next, Jesus teaches us that we can ask and expect God to provide for each one of our needs. The phrase *daily bread* serves as a reminder of the Exodus story, specifically Exodus 16. After God had led the Israelites out of captivity and while they were wandering their way toward the Promised Land, God miraculously provided them with manna every morning. God's instructions were simple: "I will provide you with what you need for that day. No more. No less. That's my job.

Your job is to rest and trust in my provision. Don't worry about tomorrow's bread. Don't hold on to yesterday's bread. I will always have all that you need for today." Jesus shows us that when we pray, it's okay to ask God for what we need and to trust that he not only knows but is also faithful to provide us with exactly that. Every day.

"And Forgive Us Our Debts, as We Also Have Forgiven Our Debtors"

Jesus moves from requesting to repenting by revealing that we can come to God directly to receive the forgiveness only he can offer. This idea was shocking and new for Jesus' disciples. For more than a thousand years, forgiveness from God was typically sought by proxy, through a priest. Ceremonial sacrifices were offered. Someone was needed to intercede. But not so with Jesus. He taught that we can come directly to God to receive the forgiveness that we so desperately need.

But Jesus attached an addendum. "As we also . . ." was an assumption that just as we are free to ask for forgiveness from God, we are also free to offer forgiveness to those who sin against us. Can you imagine how freeing it would be to end your day by fully forgiving anyone who had wronged you? To have a clean slate? To not carry today's wrongs into tomorrow? This is one of the many ways we get to practice the way of heaven here on earth. We offer others the forgiveness we ask for and receive from God.

"And Lead Us Not into Temptation, but Deliver Us from the Evil One"

Jesus then teaches that we must ask God to guide and guard us against the pull and lull of temptation. James 1:13 tells us that God is not the one who tempts us—rather, the enemy, Satan, does. What Jesus is showing us here is that just as there is an enemy who tempts and attacks us, there is a God who protects and rescues us. God knows what tempts us, and *we* ought to know what tempts us! It serves us well to ask God for the protection that he perfectly provides.

Bonus: "For Yours Is the Kingdom and the Power and the Glory Forever. Amen." (NASB)

Some translations of Matthew's Gospel include an epilogue to Jesus' prayer.[2] It's the way I learned it as a child. It serves as a climactic conclusion to this powerful prayer. Jesus ends where he began by bringing us back to the fact that when we pray, we access the power and presence of a God who is in, above, and at the center of it all. It reminds us what's really going on when we pray and to whom we are talking. This line is both the point and the exclamation point of it all.

In a few short sentences, Jesus gives us a profoundly powerful and surprisingly simple way to pray. A way to come to God when we are still learning to walk with him. A way of talking with God that is both uncluttered and uncomplicated. He gives us a way to pray when we're not even sure what we should say.

MAKING A NEW NORMAL

As someone who grew up in America, I was taught the national anthem at a young age. It's something we sang at school assemblies and sporting events, and of course on the Fourth of July. As familiar as its lyrics may be, they're easy to forget. There are countless YouTube videos of singers struggling to hit the notes and remember the lyrics in front of thousands of people. It can be a ton of fun to watch people improvise lyrics to this famous song. But before you find yourself in a YouTube rabbit hole, you should answer this question: How much of the national anthem do *you* know from memory? I'll help you with the first few lines:

Oh, say can you see, by the dawn's early light,
What so proudly we hailed, at the twilight's last gleaming?

Do you know the next couple of lines? Are you sure? Were you able to get past the part about streaming ramparts? The reason the national anthem is so easy to forget is because it's filled with language and imagery that aren't commonly used anymore. Think about it. Do you even know what a rampart is? And when was the last time you "gallantly" did anything? Probably not recently.

It's possible to hear something so much that you forget it. To become so familiar with something that it loses its power and purpose. Like the national anthem, the Lord's Prayer has been recited so often that it's easy to lose the significance of what Jesus was teaching us about God, ourselves, and prayer itself.

If you're new to prayer or are looking for a fresh way to pray, I honestly can't think of a better place to start than with the Lord's Prayer. It is a powerful and personal way to pray when you don't quite know what to say. But it's important to note that what Jesus gave us was not simply a prayer to recite from memory but a lifestyle for us to embody.

So what would that look like? How can you take what Jesus taught his friends and followers and make it yours? Anne Lamott, in her brilliant and beautiful book *Help, Thanks, Wow,*[3] refined prayer down to its most simple state. She contends that just about all prayers we pray can be summed up in three words: "HELP," "THANKS," and "WOW." I suggest that you can pray the way Jesus prayed by starting with just a few words:

- *WOW.*
- *PLEASE.*
- *HELP.*
- *THANKS.*
- *YES!*

WOW

A great place to start in prayer is with God . . . not you. As I grew up attending church, I heard lots and lots of people pray. I remember one person, an older man, would begin his prayers with the longest list of names and attributes of God. "Great and gracious God . . . Maker of heaven and earth . . .

our Alpha and Omega . . . author and perfecter of our faith . . . Jehovah Jireh" (or Jehovah Nissi or Rapha or Roi, or sometimes all the above).[4] It would be two to three minutes before he even got to the meat of the prayer!

But there is something so right and rightsizing about beginning your prayer in a state of WOW. Jesus taught that you can pray simultaneously on your knees and in the arms of the Father. That you need both reverence and relationship when you come to God in prayer. One of the simplest ways for you to practice this is to start praying with the words "God, you are . . ."

> A great place to start in prayer is with God . . . not you.

God, you are holy.
God, you are here.
God, you are so beautiful.
God, you are so loving.
God, you are so patient.
God, you are _____ (you fill in the blank).

This is what Jesus taught us when he began his prayer with "Our Father in heaven, hallowed be your name." In that one sentence, Jesus declares several truths about the character and nature of God:

- *Our Father*—We have a relationship with God. We know him, and he knows us.

- *in heaven*—There is an "otherness" to God. He is with us but is greater than us.
- *hallowed be your name*—God is holy and perfectly deserving of our praise.

In his opening line, Jesus begins with WOW. He starts by declaring who God is before he says or requests anything else.

When you come to God in prayer, how can you begin with an attribute or attributes of him that you are most aware of or that you most need in that moment? Can you begin by telling him who he already knows he is? Can you start with God before you get to you? I suggest this not because God needs to hear it or has somehow forgotten who he is but because *we* so often do. When you start with a posture of WOW before God, it reminds you of who you are in relationship to him and why you are approaching him in prayer in the first place. God does not need to be reminded of who he is—you and I need the reminder. And WOW is a great way to do just that.

PLEASE

After telling God who he is, tell God what it is that you need. Whatever it is, ask him. Like WOW, your PLEASE prayers are about things that God already knows. He already knows all your needs before you do—and better than you do. Again, PLEASE is more for you than it is for God. And the invitation of prayer is to be as bold as you are specific. In Matthew 7:11, Jesus reminds us that God is a perfect parent who loves to "give good gifts to those who ask him." So why wouldn't you ask him?

Our daughter, Gigi, has no problem with being bold. She gets it from her mother. Gigi is responsible to thank God for dinner in our house. And she uses this time as an open mic to let God know all the things that she needs, wants, and expects him to do. She has prayed for specific desserts to be served. She's prayed for puppies. She's prayed for previous consequences to be lifted. She's not afraid to ask God for Christmas presents . . . in July. She has no problem saying PLEASE. I wonder . . . do *you*?

Jesus taught us that a right way to come to God is to come with what we need. You are not bothering God when you ask him to provide for you. He loves to take care of his children. He always has, and he always will. The question is, Are you willing to say PLEASE? Are you willing to take the posture of being openhearted and empty-handed? Are you willing to trust that God has all that you need and that he will take care of you, no matter what?

HELP

In the Lord's Prayer, Jesus gave us an insight into ourselves and into the heart of God. He taught that we shouldn't be afraid to ask for God's help with what we often struggle with on our own—forgiveness and faithfulness. These practices do not appear to be a struggle for Jesus, but they are for me. And my hunch is that they are for you as well.

Jesus reminds us that we need help forgiving others and

ourselves. That it doesn't come naturally. That in fact, forgiveness is supernatural. In the Lord's Prayer, we see that while God freely offers us forgiveness, we still need to ask for it. I cannot completely absolve myself of my sin—believe me, I've tried. There is no cosmic moral ledger where enough good deeds cancel out bad ones. I need forgiveness. I need to be forgiven.

Jesus also shows us that we need help being faithful to God so we aren't drawn down paths that lead us away from his best for our lives. That temptation is real. And no amount of self-will or self-discipline can do for me what God promises through the power of his presence. No matter how secret or subtle it may be, the truth is that temptation is never faced in isolation. God is with you. He is there. This is what David was working out in Psalm 139:7: "Where can I go from your Spirit? Where can I flee from your presence?"

For some of us, this may trigger unhealthy and unhelpful fear. "I can't escape God! I can't get a break! He's always watching!" But those with more experience with God don't see this as a burden at all but as a blessing. "Thank you, God . . . you are here! I am not alone. Even in the darkest places, your light still shines." They see the promise of God's presence, that he is not only *with* me—he is also *for* me. He is here to help. All I have to do is ask.

THANKS

While Jesus doesn't specifically say "Thank you" in this prayer, he does acknowledge that everything comes from and belongs to God, that it's all his. And Jesus acknowledges that God shares it with us by providing us with exactly what we need. We will explore this more later in this book, but it is helpful to note that gratitude is always a good rule of thumb. "Thank you, God, for loving me. Thank you, God, for hearing me. Thank you, God, for being with me. Thank you, God, for providing for me. Thank you, God, for forgiving me. Thank you, God, for helping me. Thank you, God, that you are God and I most definitely am not. Thank you for all the things I don't even know to thank you for" (this is the "D: All of the above" prayer)!

YES!

As mentioned earlier, some translations close out the Lord's Prayer with a powerful and poetic "Amen." I suppose we should take a moment in this book on prayer to talk about the word *amen*. Anyone who has ever prayed has likely tacked it on to the end of a prayer. But most folks don't really know what it means. It's just something we reflexively say when we pray.

Amen is rooted in an ancient Hebrew word that simply means "truth." It's a way of putting an exclamation point at the end of what you're saying, claiming in faith that God is there, that he hears you, and that he can answer your prayer. It's a truth rooted in past, present, and future realities. This is true because of who God is, what he has done, and what he can and will do. *Amen* isn't a throwaway word. It's a way of reminding yourself, at the end of whatever you just prayed, that it was worth praying for. That you are not just tossing words out into the universe like forgotten pennies into a wishing well but are communing with the God of the universe. That you have his full attention. That you can access his power and presence in real time, at any time. And that your prayer—no matter how big or small, no matter how long or short, no matter how quiet or loud—is a prayer that matters to God. Amen?

This, then, is how you can pray.

SIMPLY PRAY. PRAY SIMPLY.

If prayer feels new or foreign to you, know this: You are not alone. It's that way for everyone who sets out to pray. Remember, even Jesus' disciples didn't know how to pray. Not knowing how to pray is no reason not to pray. You can't do it wrong. The only "wrong" way to pray is not to pray. If you're worried about doing it wrong, pray about that. Tell God that you don't know how to do all this yet. Start there, and you are already on your way. The point of prayer is to pray. It's about engaging God in your everyday life. And if you're still feeling unsure, think of all the things you've already done today that you didn't know how to do at one point in your life. You used to not know how to read, and here you are. You used to not know how to drink coffee, and now, chances are high that you don't know how to *not* drink coffee. You used to not know how to talk and think about spiritual things, and here you are deepening and growing your relationship with God. Remember, everything you now know was new at some point. The same is true of prayer. And just like everything else in your life, the more you do it—the more you make prayer part of your everyday, ordinary life—the more normal and natural it becomes. This is my prayer for you: that you would simply pray.

I have a friend who sums up the Lord's Prayer this way: "Simply pray, and pray simply." Don't overcomplicate it. Don't smother it in "should." Don't make it some sort of spiritual competition with others. *Wow. Please. Help. Thanks. Yes!*—start there. You will have enough to pray for. In fact, if that's all you ever prayed, that would be enough. Prayer matters too much to let it be hijacked by fear or insecurity. Prayer is how you *start* and how you *stay* in a relationship with God. The God who made you for relationship made prayer a way for you to grow and deepen your relationship with him. Even if your prayers don't feel deep, even if they feel a little simple, the invitation is yours . . . to simply pray.

PRACTICE

The Lord's Prayer is one of the best spiritual practices for practicing prayer. It makes sense to start and stay there this week, to make the Lord's Prayer *your* prayer. Rather than mindlessly repeating the words that Jesus said, what would it look like for you to mindfully incorporate this prayer into your life? To make it your way of praying throughout the day and this week?

Here's a fun way you can do just that: Go into the calendar in your phone and set up five alarms to go off each day this week, with words from the Lord's Prayer attached to every alarm. Think of it as your personal call to prayer. You can set it up just like this:

9:00 a.m.—WOW

Stop for a minute or so, wherever you are and whatever you are doing, to tell God all the things that you are mindful of about him in that moment. Maybe your prayer will be about the weather you're having. Maybe it will be about God's faithfulness and how he's given you another new day, or about God's provision and how he has given you all that you need. It might be about God's grace or mercy and how he has yet to run out of love or forgiveness for you. Whatever it is, take a minute or so to tell God what he already knows about himself—just how amazing he is.

12:00 p.m.—PLEASE

When this alarm goes off, take a moment to bring all your requests to God. Whatever you need, tell him. It may not be the first time that you've said "Please" about this or that, and it doesn't need to be the last. It may have to do with a financial need. It may be something work related. It may be for a breakthrough in your life that only God can bring. You will know what it is, because odds are, you've been fixated on it already and have exhausted all kinds of time and energy worrying about it. Use this moment to ask God to do what only he can do in your life.

3:00 p.m.—HELP

Afternoon is typically when our days feel like they have the most risk of running off the rails. It can feel like work is dragging on. It can feel like the kids have found your last nerve and are holding it hostage. It can feel like school will never end. This is a great time to ask for help. Invite God to come alongside you wherever you feel like you're drowning. Lean into your neediness. Claim your dependence on God. Remind yourself that you are his child and that he is a perfect parent who loves to come alongside his children and help them become all he created them to be.

6:00 p.m.—THANKS

Our family has a practice of praying before each meal. Lots of families do. It's a simple practice of giving thanks. But rather than going through the motions of thanking God for the otherwise expected things (this day, this meal, the hands that prepared it), what if you took it up a notch and consciously thanked God for EVERYTHING that comes to mind, being as specific as possible? Thank him for big and small things from that day. Take a moment to inventory God's provision, and name those things out loud to him. Stop running, stop revving, stop resisting, and simply stop to say, "Thanks."

9:00 p.m.—YES!

As the day closes, take a moment to simply say YES to God. *Yes, I believe that you are with me! Yes, I believe that you hear me! Yes, I believe that you can! Yes, I believe that you have been faithful! Yes, I believe that you will be faithful!* YES! Rather than ending your day by numbing out, distracting yourself, or stirring up a stew of fear and anxiety, end your day by claiming the confidence that comes from knowing God. YES! I may not know how it's all gonna work out, but I know you, God. I may be amid uncertainty, but I am certain that you are with me and for me. I may not feel like I can make it, but I know that you made me and call me your own. What a powerful way to reframe whatever the day may have thrown at you. Go to sleep knowing that God is with you and will watch over you while you sleep and eventually enter a new day.

This exercise may seem simple or even a little silly at first, but think about all the other things that fill your calendar and your life. Some things are expected; others are uninvited. Rather than allowing your day to be controlled by your circumstances, you are choosing to take back your day and your thoughts with prayer. I did this little exercise of prayerful calendaring not too long ago, and I can't begin to tell you what a difference it made. It shifted my perspective. It re-centered me. It detangled me from what I thought were the demands of my life. And it gave me a way to simply pray and pray simply. Whether you're new to prayer or not, this is a powerful way to pray, one that can radically reframe and reorient your heart and mind.

PRAYER

Jesus,

Thank you for giving me a way to pray when I don't
know what to say.

Thank you for teaching me just as you taught your
disciples.

Help me not to overcomplicate prayer.

Remind me that you are not seeking perfection in prayer
but have given me an invitation to transformation
through prayer.

Thank you that you know me.

Thank you that you love me.

Thank you that you hear me.

Thank you that you are with me.

Thank you that even as I pray this prayer,
you are teaching me to pray.

YES and amen!

2

WHEN I NEED TO SAY THANKS

*The worst moment for the atheist is when he is really thankful
and has nobody to thank.*

DANTE GABRIEL ROSSETTI

As a kid, my mom was big on the thank-you note. I was not.
My position was simple—I invite you to Chuck E. Cheese,
give you tokens, and feed you something that resembles
pizza—and you give me a gift. Quid pro quo. It's a fair
exchange. No need to fill out any paperwork.

This was not my mother's position. If she had it her way,
I would be writing thank-you notes before the presents were
even opened. Now, as a parent, I am big on thank-you notes
too. As I write this, a stack of thank-you notes from our
daughter's recent birthday sits on our kitchen counter. It looks
like my mom's efforts to instill gratitude in me got through!
(Note to self: Write Mom a thank-you note for that).

Why do we make such a big deal about thank-you notes? Why do parents incessantly insist that their kids say please and thank you? Maybe it has something to do with the fact that selfishness is hardwired into our DNA . . . and gratitude is not. Gratitude needs to be taught—selfishness does not. As a baby, all you were was selfish. This is not a judgment; it's just science. Your very survival depended on you demanding what you wanted. Making your needs and wants known was your number one priority. No one had to teach you how to do that. You and I came out of the womb selfish. Words like *mine* and *now* were your native tongue, while phrases like *thank you* felt like a foreign language.

So parents teach manners and repeat it. Teach it and repeat it, all the while hoping that some semblance of gratitude will stick. It's also how we teach kids to pray. Maybe you grew up in a home that prayed before meals (or specifically, before dinner). If so, what did you call that before-meal prayer? *Grace.* That word alone is meant to remind us that everything is a gift from God, and we should say thank you. For those of us who grew up praying before dinner, that's what we did. "Thank you, God, for this day." "Thank you for this food." And one of my personal favorites, "Thank you for the hands that prepared it." Not the person, not the whole body, just the hands. The legs? Nah. The heart? Pass! We're just here for the hands.

Those simple little prayers of grace, as limited in scope as they may be, are further evidence of how each of us has a need to say thanks—and how each of us needs to be reminded to say thanks. So how do we do that with God? How do we learn to say thanks for the simple things, the obvious things, the important things, the difficult things, and the challenging things? How do we put into practice what our parents wanted us to get . . . and that we so often forget? How do we say thanks to God regularly and authentically in prayer?

GRATITUDE, THE WONDER DRUG

What if I were to tell you there is a pill scientifically proven to dramatically improve your state of being—not just by giving you a temporary high but also a wholistic enhancement of your body, mind, and soul? A pill that could positively change the way you view yourself, your circumstances, and others and could make you healthier, happier, and more hopeful? Would you be interested?

What if I told you that, unlike the endless potential side effects that prescription pills have, this pill has zero negative side effects? That this pill is already on the market and you don't need to go to your doctor or a shady Russian website to order it? And that this pill is absolutely *free*?

Now are you interested?

Unfortunately, there is no such pill. But it has been proven that a daily dose of gratitude can have a profoundly positive effect on your life. An overwhelming set of data proves that gratitude has an unlimited benefit on the human condition. In their book *The Power of Thanks*, Eric Mosley and Derek

Irvine document the surprising and transformational power of gratitude. In it, they state,

> Gratitude magnifies the spirit and promotes well-being. In good times and bad, authentic appreciation creates perspective, literally stepping back from the distractions of the moment and affirming something more lasting than passing circumstance.[1]

Among their many discoveries, Mosley and Irvine found that a regular practice of gratitude changes the way we live, including how we do our work.

They also found that grateful people

- have increased emotional well-being;
- get along better with others;
- are more resilient to trauma;
- sleep better;
- are physically healthier; and
- are less depressed.[2]

There's no pill on the market that can do all that! There's no amount of positivity seminars you can attend that can accomplish this in your life. Just one little word: *Thanks.* That's a powerful little word! Gratitude radically reframes your attitude. It gives you a glimpse of the bigger picture. It lifts your head out of your circumstances and your heart toward something—and someone—greater. Gratitude reminds you that it's not all about you and that it's not all up to you. It is acknowledging unexpected or unmerited goodness directed squarely at you. Gratitude is just good for the soul.

The data is clear. The studies are conclusive. The evidence is obvious. So . . . why don't you do it more? Why is it so hard to utter that utterly simple monosyllabic word? How do you become a more grateful person—not only in life but also in prayer? How do you become fluent in the language of gratitude with God? And what do you think might happen if you did?

LIKE A LIGHT IN THE NIGHT

Few people have embodied gratitude more than Holocaust survivor Elie Wiesel. I remember reading Wiesel's seminal work, *Night*,[3] in college. I had no context for what he had endured. With suffering and death as his daily companions, it would be easy to imagine Wiesel emerging from his Auschwitz experience as a beaten down and broken man. But he emerged out of that darkness with something far different, with something much greater: He emerged with gratitude—a deep and profound sense of gratitude for life and the goodness of God, even in the face of evil.

Gratitude radically reframes your attitude.

Decades later, in a conversation with Oprah Winfrey about his experiences, Wiesel said,

Right after the war, I went around telling people, "Thank you just for living, for being human." And to this day, the words that come most frequently from my lips are *thank you*. When a person doesn't have gratitude, something is missing in his or her humanity. A person can almost be defined by his or her attitude toward gratitude.[4]

When Oprah pressed (as she often does), asking how this kind of mind-set was even remotely possible given all that he had witnessed and experienced firsthand, Wiesel replied,

For me, every hour is grace. And I feel gratitude in my heart each time I can meet someone and look at his or her smile.[5]

Gratitude is a choice. It is a conscious shift to tap into the deep well within your soul and let living water flow. Being able to recognize God even in the darkest nights and most difficult places is a gift. You have that same gift within you. It is there beneath the surface, beyond your circumstances. Like all water in all wells, it needs to be drawn out. And prayer is perhaps the greatest place to practice doing just that.

POST-IT NOTES OF GRATITUDE

Long before your parents were teaching you to say thanks, the Bible was highlighting the transformative power of gratitude. Woven throughout its pages and passages are reminders to stop and say thanks to God, to accent and underline your life and prayers with gratitude. These reminders are like Post-it notes left by those who lived for God long before you ever got here. People who struggled with prayer, just like you—and who somehow knew that we would need to be reminded to do what our hearts long to do.

Here are just a few of those Post-it notes of gratitude:

Give thanks to the LORD, for he is good;
    his love endures forever.
1 CHRONICLES 16:34

Enter his gates with thanksgiving
    and his courts with praise;
    give thanks to him and praise his name.
PSALM 100:4

Give thanks to the LORD, for he is good,
    for his steadfast love endures forever.
Give thanks to the God of gods,
    for his steadfast love endures forever.
Give thanks to the Lord of lords,
    for his steadfast love endures forever.
PSALM 136:1-3, ESV

Give thanks in all circumstances; for this is God's will for you in Christ Jesus.
1 THESSALONIANS 5:18

There is no shortage of reminders throughout the Bible for us to stop and say thanks to God. Its rhythm of gratitude serves as a reflection of and an invitation to what our lives with God could be like. And yet so often we treat gratitude like we do flossing, exercise, or drinking more water: We know that it's good for us and that we should do it, but we don't—at least not regularly. It is often and easily forgotten.

THE GOOD KIND OF EMAIL

As a pastor, I receive a lot of emails. There are the ones in which people want to know more about our church or about Jeanne and me or our family. There are the ones from other churches and organizations asking if we can partner together on this project or that. There are the ones in which people have follow-up questions about a recent message. There are the critical ones in which well-meaning folks want to let me know how and where we're getting it all wrong. (Those are fun!) There's the occasional email from the nephew of a Nigerian prince seeking our help claiming his uncle's fortune.

But then there are the ones that have no other agenda than to simply say thanks. "Thanks for pastoring a place where I found God." "Thanks for the sermon that you recently gave." "Thanks for saying yes to God's invitation to start this church." These are the emails that I cherish. These are the ones I read and then reread two or three times. These are the ones I most need when I am at my lowest. When I'm discouraged. When I feel like giving up. When I've made everything difficult or hard.

Recently, a guy in our church sent me one of these emails out of the blue. His name is John. He and his wife, Denise, have been a part of our church for years and have led and served in many different facets and capacities. John currently serves on our prayer team as the doorman in front of the prayer hall. I'm not kidding. Think of a bouncer outside a club. Now take off the sunglasses and add shorts—even when it's forty degrees outside—and that's John. He makes sure that every person gets prayed for after each of our gatherings. He's a fixture in our church.

John's email to me was simple. He just wanted to say thanks. Thanks for listening to the Holy Spirit. Thanks for creating a church where people can come as they are and have a transformational experience with God. Thanks for the sacrifices that Jeanne and I have made. Just . . . thanks. That's it. My hunch is that it took John two to three minutes to write, but it made my week. It changed my whole perspective. It reminded me why we do all that we do. I shared it with Jeanne and with our staff. I'm sharing it with you now. All that from someone not forgetting to say thanks.

Why do I tell you that story? Is it just a thinly veiled attempt to get you to send me a thank-you email? Possibly. But more than that, it's to highlight how easy and important it is to simply say thanks. To remind you of the power of that word. To underscore how saying thanks is a blessing not only to the person who receives it but also to the person saying it.

Consider the leper who received a double blessing from Jesus (Luke 17:11-19; we'll look at this story more closely later). He received not only the miraculous blessing of healing but also a verbal blessing and affirmation of his faith from Jesus. The one who had already received received even more by simply showing up and saying thanks.

And so it is with you and me. Saying thanks to God comes with a similar kind of double blessing. There is the blessing that comes from acknowledging and accepting all you have received from God in this life and seeing it as a gift: This is the first blessing. That you see it, that you have it—that's a gift. The second blessing comes from what happens in and to you when you come back and say thanks: How it changes your heart. How it grows a greater sense of gratitude. How it reframes your circumstances. That's the second blessing of saying thanks. Our transformational invitation is to practice greater gratitude in our everyday lives until it becomes as normal and natural and life-giving as . . . breathing.

Inhale—recognize God's goodness.
Exhale—respond to God's goodness.

GRATITUDE AS A SECOND LANGUAGE

I know enough Spanish to get me into trouble. I took two years of Spanish in high school and another year in college. But my real education came from a job I had during college. Most of the staff I worked with were Mexican, and they took it upon themselves to teach me all the things schools don't teach you, whether or not I wanted them to. I learned a lot—much of which I can't repeat in this book. But I'm grateful for their lessons nonetheless.

As with any language, in Spanish there are a few core words that, if learned, can get you a long way:

- hola—hello
- por favor—please
- sí—yes
- no—no
- la vida loca—the crazy life

And of course . . .

- gracias—thank you

You may not know much Spanish, but if you know some of these basic words, you can get fairly far.

So it is with prayer. If prayer makes you feel intimidated or maybe a little out of practice or even burned out a bit, you are not alone. And you know more than you think, because you know how to say thanks. You know that word. And you can always start there.

At any given moment, you can take a quick inventory of your life. Pay attention to what comes to your mind first, because this is precisely what preoccupies you. It might be your kids or your marriage. Maybe it's a difficult conversation you need to have. Maybe it's some pressure you're facing at work or the calming quiet of a house when no one else is up. Whatever it is, pay attention to it. Notice it. Name it. Let go of limiting labels like "good," "bad," "big," or "small." Just take a moment to notice what's going on *in* and *around* you. In fact, why don't you do that right now? For the next thirty seconds, stop reading this and just pay attention to your life. Don't overthink it. Just make a little list of what comes up first. I'll wait.

Okay. Got it? Good. Now, thank God for each of those things. Start with the word you already know: *thanks*. And be specific.

> "God, thank you for my children. They are a gift from you."
> "God, thank you for my job. I know that I complain about it a lot, but thank you for this source of income."
> "God, thank you for this cup of coffee. It's a small, warm comfort to me."
> "God, thank you for a refrigerator full of food."
> "God, thank you for friends who feel like family."
> "God, thank you for this book. It's helping me connect with you and helping me grow spiritually. Also, God, I pray that it sells a million copies." (I mean . . . it can't hurt.)

This whole exercise should only take a minute or so. That's it. And the more you do it, the more natural it will become to you and the more it will flow from you.

The secret to praying through every season of your life is to see every season as a gift, to know that God has something for you in all of it. God always has something good for you, no matter what your season or circumstance. Strangely enough, the practice of saying that simple little word that you already know—*thanks*—profoundly changes the way you see God, your life, your season, and your circumstances.

GROWING GREATER GRATITUDE

Our family loves gift giving. Jeanne and I delight in surprising our kids and each other with little reminders of our love. We pride ourselves on being dialed in to what our kids are interested in and what speaks love to them. And our kids are more than willing to help. For Christmases and birthdays, they essentially put together Excel spreadsheets of their lists, complete with PowerPoint presentations of what they want, where to buy it, and how much it costs. I'm sure they appreciate our thoughtfulness and intentionality, but they don't leave anything up to chance. Although we appreciate their gratitude and excitement, it seems a bit misdirected. If they should be thanking anyone, it's themselves—for making their lists so incredibly clear. All we did was serve as the middlemen between them and Amazon. A sort of gift broker.

It's not terribly hard to say thanks for the things you expect, is it? "Thank you for giving me exactly what I explicitly told you that I wanted. You know me so well." And yet when it comes to how we express our gratitude to God, we pretty much do the same thing. You ask God for something (maybe it's a new job, or more resources, or that someone with a modicum of emotional intelligence will ask you out, or a good diagnosis, or a decent parking spot), and when you get it—that exact thing that you asked for—you say thanks. This is a right and good thing to do. But there is so much more! So much gratitude is left on the table.

Not long ago, I found myself in a particularly challenging season at work. I was feeling overwhelmed. We had gone through several staff transitions in a relatively short time. I could see only all that was wrong or broken in our church. I was discouraged and defeated. I shared this with a leadership small group that I am in (by "shared," I mean whined and complained about). The group encouraged me to practice appreciation. They encouraged me to find at least ten things I appreciate about our church on that upcoming Sunday and verbally share those things with ten different people over the course of the day. I took their challenge.

The next Sunday, I made it my intention to pay more attention to appreciation. It was a little awkward at first, but it turned into a wonderful experience in no time. I told one of our production volunteers how much I appreciate her level of excellence in service. I told one of our staff members how cool and inspiring our office space is. I told one of our worship leaders that I am grateful for them and their creative leadership of our church. Before I knew it, I had blown past my goal of ten appreciations and lost count of what I was thankful for.

Those little acts of appreciation led to a big shift in my spirit and perspective! The next time the group was together, I reported back how much that experience meant to me. Their response came as a surprise. I expected a gold star for all my hard work; instead, our group leader said, "That's great, Jarrett. I'm glad that was so helpful. But it seems like your appreciations are all about obvious things. Of course you appreciate volunteers. Of course you're grateful for the music and the building. That makes sense. But what about the small things? The not-so-obvious things? The brisk morning air. Ears to hear that amazing music. The smell of fresh-brewed coffee in the café." I hadn't thought of that. He went on. "What about appreciating the challenges your church is facing right now? Or the staff who left? Or your fear that this will be the weekend that no one shows up? What would happen if you appreciated those things as well?" Now I *definitely* had not thought of that. What if I were grateful for not only the obvious things—the things that I asked for or wanted, the "positive" things—but also for everything else? What if I counted it all as joy, thanking God for it . . . for what it *is* . . . even when it's not what I want. What if you did the same?

This is how gratitude grows. This is how we learn to give thanks in all seasons. It's not by saying thanks to God when you get what you want or what you asked for, but when you learn to say thanks for *all* things; when you see it all as a gift, even the things that weren't on your list.

Let's go a little further. What about the things in your life that you don't feel grateful for—the things that you would not have chosen or the things that go unnoticed? How do you say thanks even when you don't feel grateful? What does that kind of prayer look like? It might look something like this:

"Thank you, God, for this challenging season with my teenager. I feel like I'm in over my head. Thank you that just as you have been faithful with me, even when I was a teenager, you will be faithful to my teenager."

"Thank you, God, for my job. There are a hundred things I would love to change about it, and I know I don't always feel it or say it, but thank you that I have a job and that every challenge is an invitation to greater growth."

"Thank you, God, for this headache (or sore back, or cold, etc.). Thank you for my body as a whole! This pain and suffering is a reminder of my limitations and my dependence on you. Also, I'd love for you to make it go away!"

Now I know what you might be thinking: *Thank God for a headache?!? Thank God for a sore back?!? For a cold?!? WHY?* That's a *great* question that you may or may not have asked.

Let's take the headache.

Aren't you grateful that God intricately and intentionally made your body just the way he did?

Aren't you grateful for a body that tells you to take care of it?

Aren't you thankful for a God who heals the big and small things in our bodies?

Aren't you grateful that it's only a headache?

If you answered yes to any of those questions, start there. Thank God for that. It's a lot to be grateful for. And that little act of awareness, that little shift from grumbling to gratitude can have an immeasurable effect on your outlook and how you go about your day.

I'm reminded of the child's prayer that made its way around the Internet years ago:

Dear God, thank you for the baby brother, but what I wanted was a puppy.

The ability to say thanks even when things are not as you want is a sign of true gratitude. These are powerful, perspective-shifting prayers. This isn't some half-hearted attempt to wrap a bow on challenging things; rather, it's about seeing the bow that's already there. It's a way of finding the gift from God in all things, in all circumstances . . . even if that gift comes wrapped in sandpaper. It's choosing to believe that God is good and that he works all things together for good (Romans 8:28), that even when you're at your lowest there is gratitude to find there. Like loose change in the couch cushions, it's there. It may not be easy to find. It may take some digging. But that change is there.

This is one of the simplest, easiest, and most transformational ways for you to pray your way through life.

Whatever season you find yourself in, there is always something to be thankful for. Rather than waiting until you get what you want to say thanks, start with where you are and what you have *right now*, in this moment. You can do this at *any* moment. In the morning. In bed at night. In the shower. In the car pool lane. On a walk. In your office. In the doctor's office. While the kids are napping. Really . . . anywhere. At any point throughout the day, you can take sixty seconds to name the big and small things you are grateful for. I guarantee you will not run out of things to say thanks to God for.

LEARNING FROM LINCOLN

As an American, I grew up in a culture of greed and consumerism. This isn't the whole of the American experience, but it is a lot. Perhaps this is why, as a nation, we have to remind ourselves every year to stop, if only for a long weekend, and be thankful. We dedicate two whole days off of work and school to say thanks. America isn't the only nation that attempts to express its gratitude, but it's one of the few that dedicates a national holiday to it. And while through revisionist history and a Charlie Brown special we have somehow managed to attach our nation's complicated, controversial foundation and formation to this holiday, the origin story isn't what makes Thanksgiving so interesting. It's not so much *what* we celebrate but *how* we began celebrating that's worth noting.

Thanksgiving was first made into a national holiday by Abraham Lincoln (a notorious underachiever) in 1863.[6] At the time, the US was embroiled in the American Civil War, a war that all but tore this nation and its conscience to shreds. America had seemingly very little to be grateful for at the time. The country was divided into North and South. There was a national clash of vision and ideology. Our inability to recognize the dignity and equality of the whole of humanity was and is one of our greatest national sins. The future of our fledgling democracy was up for grabs. Our nation was at its lowest when Lincoln declared that if we were ever to heal and restore our moral divide, we needed to stop and say thanks to God.

In a speech enacting this new national holiday, Lincoln said,

> The year that is drawing towards its close, has been filled with the blessings of fruitful fields and healthful skies. To these bounties, which are so constantly enjoyed that we are prone to forget the source from which they come, others have been added, which are of so extraordinary a nature, that they cannot fail to penetrate and soften even the heart which is habitually insensible to the ever watchful providence of Almighty God.[7]

Regardless of Lincoln's religious views (which continue to be studied and debated to this day), this is a profoundly *spiritual* vision. Lincoln somehow knew that gratitude had the power to change and even heal our nation. That even as war raged on, as our nation fought for its very soul, as letters were sent home confirming families' worst fears, we could . . . we *must* be thankful. That gratitude, albeit institutionalized gratitude, was the only hope we had. He wasn't wrong. It's still true.

The title of this chapter is "When I Need to Say Thanks," but perhaps a better title might be "When I Don't Feel Like Saying Thanks." Thanking God when life is not going how we want it to go is one of the most subversive and transformative things we can do. Ecclesiastes 3 teaches us there are times to grieve, to mourn, and to lament (which we will explore later in this book), but that doesn't mean we can't find and forge a spirit of gratitude to God, even in those difficult seasons. We can thank him for good things and bad things, for heavy things and light things, for wanted things and unwanted things, for all things at all times.

Our ability to thank God today greatly determines our tomorrow. We don't have to wait to say thanks until we *feel* grateful; we say thanks to *become* grateful. In other words, saying thanks isn't the outcome of gratitude—gratitude is the outcome of saying thanks. Thanking God for more and more of our lives, even when we don't *feel* particularly grateful, grows greater gratitude in our hearts over time. And it is precisely this gratitude that can carry us through difficult seasons by changing and transforming our hearts and minds. It lifts our eyes up and out of our current circumstances and helps us see that God sees and

> **Saying thanks isn't the outcome of gratitude— gratitude is the outcome of saying thanks.**

knows what we're going through—and that he is faithful. He is good and will carry us through.

RUN THAT BACK

In Luke 17, we are given a picture of how easy it is to forget to say thanks—and what happens when we do remember. Luke sets the stage for us:

> Now on his way to Jerusalem, Jesus traveled along the border between Samaria and Galilee. As he was going into a village, ten men who had leprosy met him. They stood at a distance and called out in a loud voice, "Jesus, Master, have pity on us!"
>
> VERSES 11-13

Context is everything in this case. Luke wants us to know where Jesus is and who he is with. He's on his way to Jerusalem, the center of Jewish life and worship. But he's not there yet. He's still a good way off from Jerusalem, cutting through Samaria to get there. As you may know, in Jesus' day, Jews hated Samaritans. They saw them as half-breeds, descendants of Israelites who had married and mated with their enemies. There was no love lost between Jews and Samaritans.

The group that approaches Jesus includes both Jews and Samaritans. Of this lowly lot, the Samaritans are twice cursed: They are Samaritan *lepers*, the outcasts of the outcasts. And yet Jesus is with them. Notice Luke's positioning

of players—*they* are the ones who stand at a distance from
Jesus, not Jesus from *them*. And from that distance they
yell out to him by name, acknowledging his divinity or his
humanity . . . or both. "Help us! Have mercy on us! Please,
do something."

Luke goes on:

> When he saw them, he said, "Go, show yourselves to
> the priests. And as they went, they were cleansed.
>
> LUKE 17:14

Wouldn't you know it, Jesus is merciful: His miraculous
power heals them as they are on their way.

Their healing was powerful and meaningful, but that is
not the point of this story. It's not Jesus' response to the
Samaritans that we are to pay attention to but *their* response
to him:

> One of them, when he saw he was healed, came
> back, praising God in a loud voice. He threw himself
> at Jesus' feet and thanked him—and he was a
> Samaritan.
>
> LUKE 17:15-16

All of them were healed. Only one of them returned. All
of them had been given a new lease on life. Only one of them
thought to say thanks. This one who only moments earlier

had stood at a distance from Jesus was now throwing himself at Jesus' feet. And Luke doesn't want us to miss who it was: a Samaritan. The one most despised demonstrated the most gratitude. He may not have known all the rules of social conduct. He may not have even fully known who Jesus was. He just knew that he had been given a gift and said thanks. This isn't lost on Jesus:

> Jesus asked, "Were not all ten cleansed? Where are the other nine? Has no one returned to give praise to God except this foreigner?" Then he said to him, "Rise and go; your faith has made you well."
>
> LUKE 17:17-19

Where were the other nine? Where were the others who were healed, who received the same miracle? Where were the Jews who had grown up memorizing prophecies of the one who would come to heal and to set free? Where were they? Jesus blesses the one for his gratitude, sending him into his new life.

The moral of the story is not subtle. Most of us (in this case, nine out of ten) either fail to or forget to say thanks for the big and small blessings in our lives. For the highs and lows. For the triumphs and the trials. So often, gratitude gets lost. In this story, Luke wants us to pay special attention to the fact that the people who ought to know better are often first to forget. We will never know whether the other nine people who were healed felt grateful or not. All we know is that they failed to express it. They missed out on the extra blessings given to those who remember, to people who may not know all the rules but recognize a miracle when they receive one. The nine who never returned to say thanks did not have their miracle taken away. (That would be cruel and out of character for Jesus.) But they missed out on this personal moment of blessing and affirmation from Jesus, the source of all blessings.

SPILE ON

The evidence is obvious, the outcome consistent: Gratitude changes us. It gets our eyes off our circumstances and onto God. It helps us see not only the bigger picture but also a *better* picture: that there is more. That God is good. And that there is something within all of us, deep down, that knows and must express that. Gratitude is there, but it must be drawn out.

Now, I'm not a camper. I don't like hiking. Glamping is even a bit much for me. But there is a small tool used by seasoned campers and hikers that can make a huge difference when water isn't present. It's called a *spile*: a sharp funnel that can be used to draw sap or water. Find the right tree, hit the right spot . . . and water begins to flow.[8] Water from a tree. This small, innocuous tool has saved many hikers' lives.

Prayer is a spile. It taps in, even through the rough and coarse circumstances of life, to that place within us where gratitude awaits. It connects us to that place. It connects us to God. What flows from prayers of gratitude not only blesses us but also blesses others—and ultimately blesses God. Sometimes prayer flows naturally and easefully. Other times prayer comes only after a hard-won fight. But praying is always worth it. It is worth pushing through. Praying through is worth it because what's always on the other side is a deeper and more expansive life with God.

PRACTICE

We have a funny way of rewriting history, especially our own. Perhaps history keeps repeating itself because we keep rewriting it. What if we could take something we're already good at (rewriting history) and transform it through prayers of gratitude?

At the end of the day, take five minutes to rewind your day while it's still fresh. Think through your highs and lows. In prayer, thank God for each of them. Thank God for the things you missed in the blindness of your busyness (a moment at breakfast with your kids, a conversation with a coworker) or even the stress of a deadline that you're under. See if you can find something to thank God for in the difficult things of your day.

And like a spile, press in deeper. Don't just thank God for the event or the person or the surface details; thank him for the deeper things. For the things you learned about yourself. For the things you learned about God. Look for

God in all of it because—I promise you—he was in *all* of it. And when you find him, thank him. This small, simple practice helps you rewrite your history with a greater sense of gratitude and a deeper connection to God.

PRAYER

Good and great God,

Help me to be more grateful.

Thank you that you are for me.

Thank you that there is always a gift for me, even if it's wrapped in sandpaper.

Thank you for working all things together for my good— even the things that I don't choose.

Thank you for the good and bad, the big and small, the wanted and unwanted, the named and unnamed things in my life.

Thank you that by praying this prayer, I am well on my way to a life of greater gratitude.

Amen.

3

WHEN I NEED HELP

If prayer is the heart of religion,
then petition is the heart of prayer.

HERBERT H. FARMER

There are a few schoolyard games that somehow seem to transcend time. In a time of iPhones and Xboxes, kids still gather at recess to play some of the classics. There's

Tag;
Red Rover;
Capture the Flag; and
Steal the Bacon (sadly, rarely played with *real* bacon).

And of course, Mother May I. Did you ever play Mother May I growing up? It's a cruel and sadistic game. The rules are as follows:

A power-hungry demigod deems himself or herself MOTHER, which is enough to get Freud's attention.

Everyone else is forced to plead with MOTHER to do anything. "Mother, may I take three baby steps?" or "Mother, may I take two giant steps or four scissor steps?" And so on.

Then MOTHER, depending solely on his or her mood in the moment, grants or denies the requests until eventually, someone crosses the finish line and in turn becomes the next "mother," only to dole out to others what they just endured

This game is the stuff that great counseling appointments are made of. It basically teaches kids that power is a fickle thing and the only way to get what you want is to catch mother in a good mood. We called this "fun" when I was a kid.

As odd a game as Mother May I is, this is often how we approach God in prayer, especially when it comes to asking for what we need. We close our eyes, cross our fingers, and hope to catch God in a good or generous mood.

"FATHER, MAY I have a new job?"
"FATHER, MAY I have enough money to make ends meet?"
"FATHER, MAY I have a better marriage?"
"FATHER, MAY I meet someone to spend the rest of my life with . . . preferably before my life ends?"

We ask God for the things we want or need, unsure whether he can or will give them to us. Fear strong-arms faith in small, subtle ways and leaves us wondering if God really knows or cares. Fear can make us wonder if we're too selfish for wanting what we desire, so we don't even ask. Or if we're asking for the wrong things—or for the wrong reasons. This in turn can lead you to ask God for something you really want or need when all the while you're preparing a backup plan in case he doesn't come through.

It's all too easy to get yourself all tied up in spiritual knots over something intended to be simple. Going back to the Lord's Prayer, we see that the second part is simple: It's PLEASE. After Jesus teaches us to start with God's glory and goodness, it is a right and good thing to say please. That's what "Give us today our daily bread" (Matthew 6:11) means. It's acknowledging that we have needs. Daily needs. Big and small. For us and for others. And God expects us to ask him to meet those needs. After all, this is how Jesus prayed. Jesus, who had everything he needed and could do anything he wanted, still asked God for help. Why should we pray any differently?

The real work for me—and I imagine for you—is learning *what* to ask for and *how* to ask for it. How do I know what I really need? Is it okay to pray for things that I want? How many times should I ask God for something? What do I do while I'm waiting for God's help? Does God hear me when I pray for the Cubs? Does it make a difference? These are profoundly spiritual questions. They are significant, but they are not as complicated as you might think. You already know a lot about asking for help. The challenge in prayer is the same as that of life: Will you ask for help—for what you need—and will you believe that God can and will do something about it?

Together, if you're ready, let's take three scissor steps forward in prayer.

ASK EARLY. ASK OFTEN.

As I stood at the bottom of the basement stairs looking up at my wife, my feet covered in what I could only assume was toxic waste, I realized that I maybe, just maybe should have asked for help.

It was our first home—a little two-bedroom, one-bath house that we made our own. We decided to finish the basement by adding a family room, bedroom, and bathroom. We were going to do it on our own—without professional help. With some assistance from Jeanne's dad and a plumber friend from church, we began to jackhammer the floor to install the new rough plumbing.

I realize now that after the jackhammer broke through the floor and fell about two feet into what was supposed to be solid ground, I should have been concerned. Apparently the old clay pipe that carried away everything that gets flushed had broken many years before we bought the house. Meaning . . . everything that was supposed to be flushed away over the last decade or so had just been hanging out, waiting to be discovered like an Indiana Jones–esque ancient artifact. It was not a pleasant discovery. And much like in the first Indiana Jones movie, this discovery almost melted my face off.

As I look back now, I can see that this would have been a great time to get some professional help. Preferably from someone who knew something about plumbing, foundations, or even waste management. I should have brought in an expert. I did not.

We jackhammered the rest of the distance of the rough plumbing, and I began cleaning out and bagging up the mess so we could keep working the next day. Begrudgingly, I went to the hardware store and purchased the following items:

- industrial trash bags
- industrial bleach
- industrial gloves
- industrial masks
- a nonindustrial shovel (to be thrown away immediately afterward)

I won't tell you about how the maggots sounded like four hundred bowls of Rice Krispies being eaten simultaneously. Or about how drowning them and dousing everything in that personal portal to hell with eight gallons of bleach caused my eyes to water for almost an hour. I won't tell you about how high-top skate shoes aren't really designed for that kind of work. Or about how as soon as Jeanne came home and saw what had happened, she immediately walked out of the house for some important errand that she had just remembered. All I'll tell you is that if you ever find yourself filling twelve industrial garbage bags full of the funk of forty thousand years, it's always a good idea to double bag. ALWAYS DOUBLE BAG. Because I wish someone would have told *me* that.

Jeanne arrived right as I finished excavating. All the bags were loaded, ready to be carried up the stairs to a rented truck and driven to the dump (please note that I am avoiding several jokes right here). Again, this would have been a great moment to ask for help. I did not. Instead, I decided to cut my loading time in half by grabbing not one but two bags at a time, throwing them over my shoulder. Each bag weighed about forty pounds.

I began to walk toward the basement stairs. I hadn't even put a foot on the first step when I heard a sound that I will never forget: a zip that was both fast and furious. With Jeanne looking down from the top of the stairs, I suddenly felt a weightlessness from the bags and a heaviness within my heart—and on top of my feet. The entire contents of both bags were lying at, on, and around my feet. I was speechless. Jeanne was speechless. All of heaven was speechless. Without even saying a word, Jeanne simply turned around and walked out the door. I can't say that I blame her.

Clearly, I needed help. Not just with this task but mentally and emotionally as well. There were several points throughout this experience where I could—and *should*—have asked for help. Several moments where I could have reached out to others and asked them to step in. Several moments where I could have admitted that I was in over my head (or in this case, my shoes). But because of embarrassment, or overassessing my skills, or not wanting to bother or burden anyone else, I didn't. And I paid the price. This is so often how many of us ask God for help. We have multiple chances to ask for God's assistance with various things happening in our lives. Daily decisions and dilemmas present opportunities to invite the God of the universe into our little world. And often, for many different reasons, we simply don't.

VOTE EARLY. VOTE OFTEN.

I'm from Chicago. Our city is America's political reality show. We're the city that has a history of paying folks for their vote . . . and then paying them to vote in place of their recently deceased relatives.[1] We're the city that invented the phrase "Vote early. Vote often."[2]

The political implications of this phrase are admittedly problematic, but it's actually a fitting sentiment when applied to prayer and asking God for help.

Pray early. Pray often.

Ask early. Ask often.

Before making a decision that you will regret later. Before your life hits a wall. Before you forgo faith and fall back on your backup plans. Before lifting eighty pounds of raw sewage by yourself. Before it's too late. Ask!

When it comes to God, prayer, and naming needs, ask early. Ask often.

ASKING . . . SEEKING . . . KNOCKING . . .

Praying for help is our primal prayer. In many ways, it is our entry point to prayer. Something deep down in our souls admits that we *need* help. And something in us assumes or at least hopes that God *can* help—for good reason.

The Bible is filled with invitations to ask. Jesus famously says in Matthew 7:7-8,

> Ask and it will be given to you; seek and you will find; knock and the door will be opened to you. For everyone who asks receives; the one who seeks finds; and to the one who knocks, the door will be opened.

Here we see both permission and a promise: You can ask, and God will answer. Jesus doesn't put any clauses or conditions on this statement. There's no good-deed deductible to pay off before God starts to move. No minimum-spiritual-age requirement. Just the unsettling assurance that God is open and available to you asking.

Jesus goes on, giving us a window into how good God is. He says,

> Which of you, if your son asks for bread, will give him a stone? Or if he asks for a fish, will give him a snake?
>
> MATTHEW 7:9-10

Jesus isn't a parent himself, but he knows a lot about parenting. Specifically, he knows a lot about *bad* parenting. Jesus asks the obvious question: What kind of parent would do that? What kind of parent would give a stone? That's a terrible gift. What kind of parent, when packing a child's lunch, decides to forgo the baloney sandwich and tuck a snake in the Tupperware instead? That's just cruel. Funny, but cruel.

When I was seven, all I wanted for Christmas was a transistor radio. I wanted to listen to "Weird Al" Yankovic on my own terms. I was very clear about my request. Weeks before Christmas, I circled it in the catalog (back when we used to print out Amazon search results), drew arrows to it, and dog-eared the page before giving it to my parents. I had teed up Christmas for them. It was theirs to fail. Well, imagine how I felt when I unwrapped my last present that Christmas morning only to find a pack of nine-volt batteries. That's it. Just . . . batteries. Who gives *batteries* as a Christmas gift?!? I tried to act grateful. But I was crushed.

> Praying for help is our primal prayer. It is our entry point to prayer.

My dad asked, "What? I thought you liked batteries. You can use them with so many things! It's a great gift!" He went on for a minute or two, commenting on what a great and practical Christmas gift it was. I tried to put on a smile. But before a tear started to form in my eye, he reached behind the couch and pulled out one last secret gift. The last *last* gift, one that he had hidden. He looked and me and said, "Maybe you could use those batteries with *this*?" I ripped open the paper to find my very own transistor radio! The exact one I had circled, highlighted, and dog-eared. How did they know?!?

They knew because that's what good parents do. This is the point that Jesus is making. In fact, he puts an exclamation point on this point by saying,

> If you, then, though you are evil, know how to give good gifts to your children, how much more will your Father in heaven give good gifts to those who ask him!
>
> MATTHEW 7:11

God is your perfect parent. He knows what you need. He knows how to help. He doesn't fumble. He doesn't fail. He will take care of you. That's a promise, one that is echoed in James 1:17:

> Every good and perfect gift is from above, coming down from the Father of the heavenly lights, who does not change like shifting shadows.

God is not only ready and willing to help when you ask but has already helped and blessed you in ways that you never even thought to ask for—countless ways that are often unseen and underappreciated. If you stopped to consider all the blessings and provisions in your life, all the ways God has come through for you, taken care of you, and spared you, I suspect that list would far outnumber any list you may have of unasked or unanswered prayers. If you reflected on that list, I believe your heart would grow in gratitude—and in confidence to ask God for exactly what you need.

GOD HAS A HISTORY OF HELPING

The Bible is filled with story after story of God meeting needs. Sending help. Doing what only he can do when people were done and undone by whatever they were facing.

Abraham and Sarah pray for a child, and despite their own impatient and imperfect plan, God still provides them with a son (Genesis 15:2; 17:15-17; 18:1-15; 21:1-6).

God provides manna, quail, and water for the people of Israel amid their wilderness wandering (Exodus 16:1-34; 17:1-5).

In a very Disneyesque moment, an exhausted Elijah is fed by ravens in the desert. And when Elijah stumbles into a town and asks a woman for some bread, only to find out she is about to make her last loaf before starving, God provides her with an endless supply of oil and flour to keep her, her son, and Elijah alive (1 Kings 17:2-16). (I can only assume this is where Olive Garden came up with their idea for end-less breadsticks.)

When Daniel faces hungry lions in a cave, he prays for God to protect him, and Daniel leaves without a scratch and with new feline friends (Daniel 6:1-28).

Hannah prays and pleads for God to give her a son, and he does (1 Samuel 1:9-28).

God protects and provides for David as he runs for his life from a murderously jealous King Saul (1 Samuel 23:14).

After moral failure upon moral failure, Samson cries out for God to give him one last bit of strength to bring justice to his enemies, and God does (Judges 16:28-30).

Gideon lays it all on the line, asking God for a sign that he will deliver Israel yet again, and God gives him the sign that he seeks (Judges 6:1-39).

Jonah prays for God to spare his life and deliver him from the belly of a great fish (a prayer that we have all prayed at one time or another), and God does (Jonah 2:1-10).

And on and on and on. The Bible is filled with helpless people calling out to a God who helps. A God who rescues. A God who provides. A God who is there. A God who has a history of helping and is just waiting for you to ask.

WHAT WE ARE REALLY ASKING FOR

When it comes to asking God for help, there are really two different *things* we're asking for and two different *people* we're asking for. And while one prayer doesn't matter more than another to God, understanding the difference between asking for *needs* and *wants* and the difference between asking for *yourself* and *others* can be helpful.

Needs and Wants

Let's explore that first one for a bit. Understanding the difference between needs and wants is incredibly important in prayer and in life in general. It's one of the primary lessons your parents tried to teach you for most of your childhood. Of course, none of us wanted to learn this lesson, but all of us needed to. We still need to, because there *is* a difference. For example,

- clothes = need
- $370 pair of retro Nike Air Jordan 1s = want
- sleep = need
- sleeping in = want
- shelter = need
- a three-hundred-foot yacht to cruise around the Amalfi Coast with Jay-Z and Beyoncé = want
- food = need
- Portillo's chocolate cake = want (although I can make a case that this is a need)[3]

You get the point. The same is true in prayer. There are things that you want and things that you need. We don't always need what we want. And we don't always want what we need. We may have a hard time telling the difference between the two, but thankfully God does not. He knows what you want *and* what you need. And he is able to give you both . . . although maybe not in the ways you expect.

God's promise to provide for all your needs is abundantly clear throughout the Bible. His willingness to give you what you want is a little different. Psalm 37:4 says, "Take delight in the LORD, and he will give you the desires of your heart."

At first glance, this promise can seem like a golden ticket. God wants to give me what I want. Great! But read it again. Look at those first couple of words: "Take delight in the

LORD." Enjoy God. Rest in God. Revel in God. Let God be what you want *first*. Let him be what you want *most*. So often I find that I want the things that I want more than I want God, and all I really want God to do is give me what I want. It's easy to believe that a newer car with better features will give you true delight. Or that a bigger house in a better school district will bring you what your heart truly longs for. Or that more money at the end of the month is all that you really need. None of these things are wrong or bad in and of themselves—it's just that so often we get them out of order. We elevate the delight we believe they will give us above the delight we already have available to us in God.

This is where *contentedness* comes in. Contentedness is perhaps one of the least sexy words in the English language. It feels like settling. It feels like something that only desert monks are capable of. But that's exactly what it means to "take delight in the LORD." This verse is an invitation for your soul to be at rest with who God is and to joyfully enjoy what you already have, with what God has already provided. To be grateful for it. To have soul-level satisfaction with what you already have.

> We don't always need what we want. And we don't always want what we need.

Embracing contentedness is about as countercultural a thing as you can do. Consumerism is predicated on discontentedness, where delight is an ever-moving goalpost. But God says that when you come to him in prayer, you should "take delight in the LORD," knowing "he will give you the desires of your heart." Start with delight, and from there, see what's left.

When God promises to give you the desires of your heart, he means it. But what God wants to give you is so much more than just what you want. I remember hearing my friend Pastor Doug Pagitt teach on Psalm 37:4 years ago. He said that while it's true that God longs to give you the desires of your heart, another way of looking at this verse is to see that God wants to give you the *right* desires in your heart. That God is far more interested in your transformation than in your wish fulfillment. He wants to give you and grow in you the kind of desires that align with *his* heart. He wants to teach you how to want the right things: The things that lead to life. The things that lead to greater peace and purpose. The things that won't disappoint or fade away.

Again, this teaching doesn't mean that I don't ask God for what I want. Often this is where my prayers start. And God loves to hear them. He loves when I bring my wants to him. And sometimes God gives me what I want. Other times he gives me so much more. He gives me the right kind of wants—ones that better reflect his heart. And in the end, isn't that what you *really* want?

Yourself and Others

So there's the difference between asking God for what you *need* and what you *want*. Then there's the difference between asking something of God for *yourself* and for *others*.

Asking God for help for yourself is called *petitionary prayer*.

Asking God to help others is called *intercessory prayer.* One is not more important than the other. Both are essential. Both are defined by dependence on God, and both are modeled throughout the Bible. In fact, the way Jesus taught us to pray (which we explored at length earlier in this book) beautifully incorporates both. The invitation is to pray for very real and very personal needs—food, forgiveness, guidance—but it's all framed in the context of "us":

"Give *us* this day . . ."
"Forgive *us* . . ."
"Lead *us* . . ."

Jesus doesn't once use the words *me* or *them.* Just *us. Us* is the beautiful brilliance of both. He invites us to pray for very real needs that you have for yourself—and to pray the same for others, to include others and their needs as you pray for yours.

We've already discussed the power and importance of praying for your needs, but it's also important to pay attention to what praying for *others* does to *you.* Praying for others . . .

Connects you to others. We live in a world where we are tangentially connected to more people more than ever before, but our connections tend to be more wide than deep. Following people on Instagram and liking their posts is fine and good, but it doesn't connect you to someone like prayer does. When you pray for someone who is sick or who needs a job or who is grieving a loss, you become their spiritual advocate and ally. You move from being *with* them to being *for* them. Praying for someone deepens your care for and connection to that person, even if there are miles between you.

Settles your selfishness. I can be a pretty selfish person. A friend and mentor once told me that I can be "sneaky" with my selfishness. In other words, I find one way or another to get what I want. *Ouch*—and spot-on. But when I take others' needs to God in prayer, my perspective shifts. It gets bigger and better. It moves beyond me. Simply taking the time I could be using for me and spending it thinking about and praying for others is, in and of itself, an act of selflessness. And that's saying nothing about what God does to me and my heart as I pray for others, or what he does for the people I pray for—simply because I chose to pray for them.

Eliminates your "enemies." I don't like to think of myself as having many enemies. I'm a pretty nice guy. I'd be a mediocre rapper at best, simply due to my lack of haters (among other necessary skills). But any time I harbor anger, resentment, jealousy, or envy toward another person, I make them my enemy, whether they know it or not. The same is true for you. One of the best ways I've found to eliminate my enemies is not by creating a diss track but through prayer. When Jesus said to "love your enemies and pray for those who persecute you" (Matthew 5:44), he meant it. One of the most powerful ways to love your enemies, those difficult people in your life, is to pray for them. Pray for God's best for your boss. Pray for God's blessing on your ex. Pray for peace between you and your sister. You simply cannot pray for someone and keep them your enemy.

Here's a good strategy for helping others through prayer (you might want to write this down):

1. Ask people how you can specifically pray for them.
2. Actually pray for them.

That's it. It is a profound privilege to pray for others. Unfortunately, it has become a sort of Christian cliché to tell someone that you're going to pray for them. Far too many people far too many times have said, "Mmmm (eyes half squinted, evoking sincerity). I'm going to pray for you, _____ (brother/sister/friend/pastor/etc.)," only to not actually pray for them. Don't be that person. When somebody asks you to pray for them or you offer to pray for them, it's always good to actually *do* it. How you do it is up to you.

I have a friend who adds to a note he keeps on his phone every time he offers to pray for someone. My grandmother once told me that she regularly prayed through every member of her family, right on down the line. When our kids were little, we kept their class pictures up on the fridge. When we sat down to eat breakfast, we picked a classmate and prayed for them.

I have built the habit of not waiting until later: Right after I say that I'll pray for someone, I pray for them. I do this not because I am some sort of super spiritual person but because I have terrible short-term memory and will most likely forget to do it five minutes later (please pray for me about that).

The point is, pray however you like; just make sure you do it. Intercessory prayer is a profound way to connect you to God and others. It has the power and potential to change your heart—and their lives.

HE'S HERE. HE HEARS.

In an age of social media that can connect you in both trivial and meaningful ways with people around the world, the idea of the pen pal has become a relic of a pre-digital history. For those born after the days of the dial-up modem, pen pals were friends you may not have met, typically from another city, state, or country. These friendships were based solely on the quality and quantity of physical letters you wrote to each other. You got to know each other line by line, letter by letter (each of which was typically written in cursive).

When I was in third grade, my teacher, Mrs. Lopez, had an idea to localize our pen pals. She had us all write letters describing ourselves and our favorite thises and thats, and then we provided our home addresses, with the invitation to write back. In hindsight, this was a bold move—I don't even like giving out my personal email address to strangers!

Mrs. Lopez had a creative twist up her sleeve. She had rented a helium machine and bought a bag of balloons. We were going to give these friend requests wings! We went out to one of the fields at our school and released our letter balloons together. It was all very exciting. Who knew where God would take these letters? Secretly I prayed that mine would be found by a spy or a stuntman and that we would become best friends. All of us went back to class, hearts filled with hopeful expectation.

That hope only lasted until school ended. As I walked home that day, I noticed balloon after balloon stuck in the tops of trees or prickly bushes just past our school grounds. Several had already popped, and their letters dangled beyond the reach of our most elevated expectations. At best, only 30 percent of our balloons made it into the wild that day. If you've ever wondered why we don't really do balloon releases anymore, this is why. And I must note, with a sad and heavy heart, that no spy or stunt person ever wrote me back.

It's so easy to see your prayers, especially your prayers for help, as balloons released into the open sky. We write our requests down, let them go, and hope that they reach heaven. We hope to hear back from a God who is somewhere up there and somehow cares. But what we see again and again in stories throughout the Bible—and what we often miss in our stories—is that God is not so much "up there" or "out there" as he is "right here." The writer of Psalm 46 tells us at the beginning of the passage that

God is our refuge and strength,
an ever-present help in trouble.

And then he closes out the psalm by saying it again:

The LORD Almighty is with us;
  the God of Jacob is our fortress.

God is already near. He is already here. He is intimately acquainted with what you need. In fact, he knows your needs better than you do. God somehow simultaneously sustains the entire universe and is totally up to speed on every one of your needs. He sees you. He knows you. He loves you. You don't have to wonder or worry if you have *his* attention. The better work is to fix *your* attention on his presence. After all, this is what we practice in prayer: the presence of God. He is already right here. He is with you. He is for you. So before you even utter the words "God, I need . . . ," be comforted and encouraged by the fact that you already have all you ultimately need. You have access to and the interest of the God of the universe. He is here. He hears. Where you go from there is entirely up to you.

THE PERPLEXING PROBLEM OF PRAYER

Perhaps one of the greatest reasons we don't ask God for what we want or need is because we're afraid that he won't do it. We fear that he'll say no, that he won't answer the way we asked, or that he won't even answer at all. Unanswered prayer is perhaps one of the most perplexing parts of prayer. Why would God invite us to ask him for anything and promise us that he is listening, only to abandon us at the altar of our asking?

This is no small thing—and a big reason why some people lose their faith. Any attempt to cover this dilemma with a Christian bumper sticker only does more harm than good.

So what do we do when we come to God seeking help, and help doesn't seem to come? As a pastor and follower of Jesus for many years now, I've had a front-row seat to God's miracles and movements. I've prayed for friends facing a terminal diagnosis and seen complete healing. I've prayed for marriages that were all but over and seen them restored and transformed by God. I've prayed for friends facing year after soul-crushing year of infertility, only to later celebrate the birth of their children. I've seen God answer impossible requests with his power and faithfulness. Too many to count! And . . . I've experienced the other side of prayer as well. I've prayed for healings that never came. I've prayed for jobs that didn't emerge. I've prayed for marriages that didn't make it. I've prayed for friends to find Jesus who still haven't. While I have a lifetime of evidence of God's faithfulness, I also have a lifetime of experience with the mystery of God. I simply don't know why God does what he does or why he doesn't always do what I want him to. And any attempt to use thin theology to spackle the holes that this lack of understanding has left in my faith does a disservice to the deeper faith and trust that God wants to grow in me.

It is impossible for me to understand why God hasn't answered *all* of my honest and earnest prayers. And it's irresponsible for me to try to tell you why he hasn't answered yours. It is true that sometimes God uses your asking and waiting and asking and waiting to grow a deeper faith and deeper desires in you. It is true that sometimes God answers your prayers in unexpected ways to lead you to something far greater than you even knew you could ask for. It is true that sometimes there is sin between us and God, sin that keeps us from intimacy with God. Unowned and unconfessed sin keep us from experiencing the full blessing of God in our lives. Perhaps this is why Jesus taught us to ask for what we need and for forgiveness in the same breath when we pray.

All those things are true—and yet I still don't know why God answers some prayers and doesn't answer others in ways that we hoped for or can recognize. But I do know that right after Jesus taught us how to pray, he taught us how to keep on praying. In Luke 11:5-8, Jesus tells the story of someone banging on the door and waking up their neighbor at midnight because he had an out-of-town guest and was out of bread. The scenario is absurd. Who would do such a thing? I feel bad asking our neighbor Joan if she can throw back any one of the ninety-three Frisbees we've thrown into her yard. And that's in the middle of the day! I can't imagine banging on her door at midnight and expecting her to get up, come downstairs, and head outside to snag a rogue Frisbee. Jesus is making a point: When we are desperate, when we have no other options, even when we have knocked on the door of heaven for thirty minutes—at midnight—we must not give up, because God will respond. In one way or another, he *will* respond. Jesus' words tell us so:

Yet because of your shameless audacity he will surely get up and give you as much as you need.

LUKE 11:8

Prayer is an unapologetic act of audacity. The willingness to keep on knocking, keep on asking, keep on trusting, and keep on believing, even when you don't get what you want or in the way you want it, is the alchemy of faith *and* persistence. It means having the faith to take God up on his invitation to ask him for whatever you need—and the tenacity to hold him to it.

Prayer is an unapologetic act of audacity.

To reach out (faith) and not let go (persistence). To wade in the waters of the mystery of God while standing on the very promises of God. To not lose heart and not lose hope while holding on. Keep knocking, keep asking, keep believing—*even if* and *even after* it doesn't go your way.

IT'S WORTH MENTIONING . . .

So whether you're asking God for what you want or what you need, whether you're asking God for yourself or for others, whether God answers your prayer in the way you want or in a way you can see—or not—the point is to keep on asking; to know that God hears and that he is here. God asks you to ask him. He invites you to bring your list of things, trivial and critical and all things in between; to ask and seek and knock—and continue asking and seeking and knocking.

Our friends at Holy Trinity Brompton church in London have a practice in their weekly staff meetings. Any time anyone from their team gives an update or information about an upcoming event, ministry, or Alpha group, they stop and pray for it, right then and there. When they stop the meeting and pray like every five minutes, the part of me who likes agendas and for things to be on time goes a little nuts inside. But they stop and ask for God to move in that specific area. They ask for people to encounter God at whatever it is that was just mentioned. They ask God to provide the leaders needed for that event or retreat. They ask for an outpouring of his Holy Spirit. They don't add a prayer to the beginning of that meeting's agenda—prayer *is* the agenda!

When asked about why they run their meetings this way, they offer this simple spiritual wisdom (spoken in a perfect British accent): "If it's worth mentioning, it's worth praying for." If it's worth *mentioning*, it's worth *praying for*. In other words, if it's worth thinking about or working on, it's worth praying for. If it's worth giving time to, it's worth praying about. If it's worth worrying about, it's worth praying about. Whatever it is, it's worth praying about.

I wonder what might happen if you began to apply that same philosophy to the way you pray. In the morning, when you find yourself thinking about a big meeting later in the day, stop and ask God for what you need. As you're heading to work and find yourself fixated on someone you're mad at, stop and ask God to grow your heart. When you're up late at night paying bills and anxiety or fear creeps in, stop then and there, with your checkbook open, and ask God to grow peace and greater gratitude in your heart. If it's worth mentioning, or mumbling about, or meditating on, it's worth praying about.

Rather than letting a day's worth of prayer pile up, stop as you begin to think about what worries you, no matter how big or small—and pray. I imagine that if you did, you would grow a greater awareness of God's presence. That you would begin to see and experience that he is with you and for you at all times. I believe that you would grow more comfortable being specific with what you need from God. That over time, you would learn to discern needs from wants. And that God would grow better, deeper desires in your heart that more align with his. As you think about it, pray about it. As you begin to stress about it, pray about it. As you begin to take matters into your own hands, take them to God in prayer. I honestly can't think of a bolder, more audacious thing you could do.

PRACTICE

Have you ever gone back and read something you wrote when you were younger? Maybe it's an old paper you wrote in college or a Mother's Day card you gave to your mom when you were seven (that she still has for some reason). It's such a fascinating experience. Jeanne and I still have the first letter I wrote her after we met. It's more than twenty-five years old. Every couple of years, we pull it out and read it.

Parts of it are embarrassing (mostly my spelling and penmanship), parts of it are beautiful, and all of it is amazing, considering that we are still together all these years later. So much has happened in our relationship since that letter. But none of it would have happened without that letter. It is a living testimony of the mystery of God's love and faithfulness.

Having a living record of your prayers works much the same way. Having a place where you can jot down what you ask God for, that you can come back to again and again, serves as a powerful prayer tool. This week, practice taking a little pocket-size notebook with you everywhere you go. Or if you're more tech-savvy, create a note on your phone. Every time you find yourself wanting something or needing something from God, write it down. Do it throughout the day. You can either pray for it in that moment or go through the list at the end of the day. Do it for a week. At the end of the week, look back. Look for God's faithfulness. Look for how you saw God answer your prayers. Look for how you saw God deepen and realign your desires. And look for what you want to carry over into the next week. Do it for two weeks . . . a month . . . a couple of months, and you will have ample evidence for both the faithfulness and the mystery of God. My hunch is that over the course of that time, you will find God has grown your heart for prayer far more than you might have realized or could have imagined.

PRAYER

Good and giving God,

you ask me to ask.

You invite me to invite you into every want and need that
I may have.

Help me to do just that.

This prayer is my asking you to help me ask you for what
I want and need in prayer.

Give me greater desires in my heart.

Help me to see your faithfulness and to settle into your
mystery.

Bring to mind the names of others, that I may love them
more purposefully in prayer.

Help me to see that you are always here and that you
always hear.

I need you more than I could ever know.

And you love me more than I could ever know.

Help me to get better at accepting both.

Because you are good.

Amen.

4

WHEN I AM WORRIED

No one can pray and worry at the same time.

MAX LUCADO

No one likes to think of themselves as a worrier. But everybody worries.

Some folks worry about the future. Some folks worry about the present. Some folks worry about their kids. Some folks worry about their parents. Some folks worry about the money they have. Some folks worry about the money they don't have. Some folks wear worry on their sleeves. Some folks are high-functioning worriers. We all worry about different things, but we all worry.

If you want to see me worry, go on a flight with me. I don't worry about the flight itself—which, when you stop to think about it, makes total sense to worry about: Let's cram two hundred people into a ninety-thousand-pound tin can and shoot them through the air at six hundred miles per hour. We'll let them breathe recycled air, and we won't feed them. Oh, and some people will take their shoes off.

If you're going to worry about something, flying makes sense. But instead I worry about everything leading up to the flight. I worry about checking in at the right time to try to get a good seat (thanks for that, Southwest). I worry about leaving the house with enough time to account for the traffic that may or may not exist. I worry about the security process taking too long. I worry about missing my flight. I worry about the flight being cancelled if there's even a hint of inclement weather. I find a way to worry about every aspect of flying except the flying part, which makes me a real *joy* to travel with.

Now, I would never call it worry. I rebranded that years ago. I call it "planning" or "being responsible." It sounds less neurotic when I frame it that way. But regardless of what I call it, it's worry, plain and simple. And it has a powerful effect on just about every aspect of my being. My mind can get preoccupied with all the variables I need to account for. If I am running late for a flight, my heart starts to beat a little faster. I grind my teeth. When I start feeling stress and anxiety, I can get short with my words. And I have been known on occasion to tell Uber drivers to act like we just robbed a bank. Worry is a toxic fog that begins in your mind and creeps its way through every crack and crease of your body and soul.

To be human is to know worry in some form or facet. If

you think you don't worry about anything, you should be worried that you don't worry about anything, because worry is actually a sign of faith—it's just fixated on the wrong things.

WORRY IS A WEED

There's an old fable about a man who came face-to-face with the dangers of worry. The story goes something like this:

One morning, a man was working by the city gates when he saw Death walking toward his city. This gave him great concern.

The man asked Death, "What are you on your way to do?"

Death answered, "Today, I am going to take the lives of one hundred people from your city."

"That's horrible! How can you do such a thing?" the man demanded.

"Well," Death told him, "that's what I do. My name is Death, after all. It's literally the only thing on my job description."

Panicked, the man frantically ran ahead to the city and warned everyone of Death's plan.

That evening, he met Death again.

"YOU LIED!" he yelled. "You told me you were only going to take one hundred people. Why did one thousand people die?"

"Oh, I kept my word," Death replied. "*I* only took one hundred people . . . *worry* took the rest."

This is how it works with worry. It adds nothing to your life—but it can ruin all of it.

Years ago, Dr. Walter Calvert did an extensive study on the power of worry in our everyday lives, funded by the National Science Foundation. More than one thousand people were interviewed about the things they worry about. The landmark study found that

- 40 percent of the things we worry about will never even happen;
- 30 percent of our worries are about the past;
- 12 percent of our worries have to do with unfounded health concerns;
- 10 percent of what we worry about and stress over are trivial, insignificant issues; and
- only 8 percent of what we worry about is connected to real issues and legitimate concerns.[1]

Did you get that? Less than 10 percent of the things you worry about concern legitimate issues. In other words, 92 percent of the things we stress over are beyond our control or will never even come to pass. Does that seem like a good exchange to you? All that time spent tossing and turning in bed at night, thinking through the next day. All the hours spent running through possible outcomes. All the energy exhausted responding to realities that will never come to be.

Worry may start in the mind, but it doesn't stop there. The

physical effects of worry and anxiety are well-documented.[2] They include the following:

- **A change in breathing and increased respiratory response.** Intense worry can lead to accelerated breathing, to the point of hyperventilation. If you've ever been so fixated on something you're worrying about that you've found it hard to breathe, then you know what this feels like.

- **Hyper cardiovascular-system response.** Worry can increase your heart rate and speed up the flow of blood throughout your body. When you're really worried, your body temperature gets warmer. As a response, the body releases sweat . . . which is why you may pit out when you're stressed.

- **Weakened immune functions.** Initially when worry or anxiety kicks in, it can boost your immune system's responses. But the longer you worry and the longer your immune system is engaged at this level, it can work against your body. Studies have found that people who experience prolonged periods of worry are more likely to catch a cold, the flu, and other types of infection.

- **Changes in digestive function.** Yep, it's true. People who carry worry in their bodies for prolonged periods have been known to experience nausea, diarrhea, and rumblies in their tummies (I believe that's the scientific term). They've also been known to lose their appetites, which can lead to unhealthy weight loss.

But the effects go well beyond the physical—they are spiritual. Worry has the power to hijack your connection to God. It can pull you out of presence with God and others. It can consume your thoughts and actions. That's because worry is a weed in the garden of faith. It can spring up overnight and grow faster than anything around it, all the while stealing precious soil and nutrients until it chokes out everything around it: things like peace, joy, patience, trust, and prayer. Trimming back worry and trying to cut it off does little more than cause it to come back even stronger. Worry, like a weed, must be uprooted—pulled up from the source—and replaced with something that bears fruit.

Worry, like a weed, must be uprooted.

THE DIRECTION OF YOUR MEDITATION

Worry weighs a ton but is worth little. It can occupy your thoughts and mind and take you out of presence with God and others. It's a way of focusing your energy and effort on something. The problem is that far too often, it's on the wrong thing and in the wrong direction.

Now, there's good news and bad news when it comes to worry. The good news is that you already know how to meditate. That's a big deal. Meditation is an incredibly important spiritual practice and is part of the deeper life of prayer. And you're already awesome at it! That's good news!

The bad news is that it's in the wrong direction.

Simply put, worry is meditation in the wrong direction. It's directing your thoughts and emotions in a way that often leads to more worry. Thankfully, there's a *better* way!

In Matthew 6:25, Jesus paints a picture of what worry is worth: where it gets you and what it takes from you.

> Do not worry about your life, what you will eat or
> drink; or about your body, what you will wear. Is
> not life more than food, and the body more than
> clothes?

Right out of the gate, Jesus is focusing our attention in the direction of things that are far bigger and more important than the little things that we tend to meditate on and worry over.

He doesn't suggest that you don't have to plan for your life or that you should avoid taking responsibility. He says not to worry about it all. I can imagine Jesus' listeners looking up into the sky as he says,

> Look at the birds of the air; they do not sow or
> reap or store away in barns, and yet your heavenly
> Father feeds them. Are you not much more valuable
> than they?
> MATTHEW 6:26

Think about it. Have you ever met a stressed-out swan? Have you ever come across a pigeon paralyzed by anxiety and inactivity? Probably not. Birds (and just about every animal, for that matter) seem to have an innate trust that their creator is also their provider. That God will take care of them. That he always has and always will. This is what Jesus wants to draw your attention to. And then Jesus gets to his point—you matter more to God than any and every bird in the sky! God cares for them, *and* he cares so much more for you.

Worry is meditation in the wrong direction.

Jesus continues by asking this simple yet transformational question:

> Can any one of you by worrying add a single hour to your life?
>
> MATTHEW 6:27

Jesus is reminding you of what you already honestly know— that all your fear and worry don't change a single thing! Worry has no external power other than to keep you from the life God has for you. It is nothing more than meditation in the wrong direction. Martyn Lloyd-Jones said it this way: "The result of worrying about the future is that you are crippling yourself in the present."[3]

Worry takes a future possibility and makes it your present reality. It takes something that might be—something that you likely have little control over in the moment—and attempts to use it to control your every thought and emotion. The truth is, no one ever worries their way to a more meaningful life, but plenty of people worry their way into a more miserable life!

Jesus doubled down on this point in Matthew 6:28-30:

> And why do you worry about clothes? See how
> the flowers of the field grow. They do not labor or
> spin. Yet I tell you that not even Solomon in all
> his splendor was dressed like one of these. If that is
> how God clothes the grass of the field, which is here
> today and tomorrow is thrown into the fire, will he
> not much more clothe you—you of little faith?

If the birds weren't enough for you to get the point of God's presence and provision, then just look at a field of flowers. They have everything they need. They trust God, and they look good doing it!

Jesus concludes by going back to the start of this teaching.

> So do not worry, saying, "What shall we eat?" or
> "What shall we drink?" or "What shall we wear?"
> For the pagans run after all these things, and your
> heavenly Father knows that you *need* them.
> MATTHEW 6:31-32, EMPHASIS ADDED

And here's the genius shift . . .

> But seek first his kingdom and his righteousness, and
> all these things will be given to you as well.
>
> MATTHEW 6:33

Do you see what Jesus is doing here? He's reprioritizing our little to-do lists! Instead of starting with all the things that we ultimately don't have any control over; instead of worrying about how it's all going to work out; instead of exhausting all our emotional energy until we finally come to God *after* we've gotten to the end of ourselves—Jesus offers the invitation *to start with God*. Seek him first. Change the direction of your meditation to him. Start by trusting that God is good and knows your needs. He knows what you've been meditating on, and he wants to remind you that he has *enough*! He has enough of whatever it is you need.

Start with God at the top of your list, and trust he will take care of everything that comes after. That is who he is. That is what he does. That is what he loves to do . . . because he loves you! The simple spiritual shift is in the direction of your attention: Will it be on the countless things you can't control or on the one who is *in* control?

This is the real work for us. All too often, we focus our attention in a thousand directions. Worry comes when we meditate on all the things that are ultimately out of our control—and lose sight of the one who *is* in control. But what if, before worry takes the wheel, we could direct our attention to God? To the powerful presence of God? To the never-failing faithfulness of God? To the providential provision of God? To the abounding abundance of God? Look at a bird if you have to! Look at a flower. Look to God first, and trust that everything worry has gotten you worked up about will be okay.

PRAYING IS JUST LIKE SNOWBOARDING

Our family loves to snowboard. Well, when I say "family," I mean me and the kids. Jeanne tried snowboarding with us a couple of years ago and within the first fifteen minutes broke her wrist. So . . . *most* of our family loves to snowboard. I learned to snowboard when the sport was still very new. The gear was terrible, and most ski resorts looked down on snowboarders. We just had to figure it out. Not so today. Our kids learned to snowboard at ages seven and nine! We enrolled them in snowboard school for a day, and they took to it like a fish takes to water (or, in this case, snow).

One of their big lessons was about turning, which, as I've learned the hard way, is important in snowboarding. The instructor taught them that the key to turning on a snowboard is turning your head. Turn your head and shoulders to the right, and your body and board will follow. Turn your head and shoulders to the left, and you can expect your body and board to do the same. Basically, your **Your attention determines your direction.** attention determines your direction. Where you keep looking is where you end up going. This is an invaluable lesson not only for snowboarding but also for anytime you find yourself worrying.

Anytime your heart and mind are fixed and focused on the one thousand things that you ultimately have no control over, you are determining the direction of your life. Your life eventually becomes all about the things you worry about. They end up occupying your thoughts, decisions, and actions. And often in the end, all your worrying and getting worked up only leaves you empty-handed and brokenhearted.

But this principle works the other way as well. Focus your attention on Jesus. Make him the one you look to and look for. Fix your heart and mind on him, and your life will follow. Your attention will determine your direction. When you start with and stay with Jesus as the object of your affection and attention, your life will be drawn more and more to him. Looking for and looking to Jesus turns your worry to worship.

THE GREAT EXCHANGE

Raising our kids in the city all these years has provided an unbelievable and unpredictable number of blessings and challenges. Our kids are city kids. They know their way around public transportation. They have grown up with a dynamic and diverse group of friends. They have an innate theology about justice for the poor and the marginalized. Sites and attractions that people travel from all over the world to experience are in their backyard. It has been a far greater experience than we could have imagined. And it's come with a unique set of challenges.

One of those is their education. Chicago has a very challenged, inequitable, and broken education system. One of the struggles of raising kids in the city is that they have to test into their high school. In other words, rather than simply attending the high school in your area, your kids must spend seventh grade taking a series of exams that will determine the type of high school they go to. Test well and get good grades, and you have a great selection of quality schools. Test poorly, and your options grow limited. On top of that, siblings have no guarantee of attending the same high school. If one tests well and the other tests poorly, they will most likely be at different schools (which, given the size of Chicago, could be anywhere from thirty to fifty minutes apart). This leaves parents in the city with a few options: (1) move out of the city, (2) spend countless time and money on tutors and test-prep courses, or (3) complain about it with each other at every birthday party, basketball game, block party, and pickup or drop-off. I never have to worry about small talk with parents of city kids. We always know what we can talk/complain about.

At the time I'm writing this, our oldest child, Elijah, is in the middle of his seventh-grade year. I can safely say that in the last two years, Jeanne and I have spent more than one hundred hours talking about high school, considering contingency plans, touring high schools, and getting advice from other parents. We still don't know what we're going to do. Saying that we have worried about our children's future is an understatement. And here's what's interesting: At the time that *you're reading* this, we will have made our decision. All that we worried about will have been worked out. We will have figured it out and moved forward . . . which makes me wonder—will this worry have been worth it?

Have you ever thought about how much time you spend worrying? How many moments? How many hours? A few years ago, a study of two thousand people in London found that we spend an average of one hour and fifty minutes a day worrying[4]—almost two hours! That's more than 8 percent of your day! And that includes all the hours you're asleep (assuming, of course, that you don't have stress dreams). Add that up, and you spend almost thirteen hours a week worrying. At this rate, over the course of sixty-five years you'll spend five years worrying. That's crazy! Five years of your life! Two hours of your day! What would you do to have those hours back? Do you think you could find a better use for that time? Something more productive? Something that's kinder to your soul? Something that moves things forward in your life?

FROM WORRY TO WORSHIP

This is God's invitation to you. He not only wants to give you your life back but also wants to give you *real* life. A life rooted in worship rather than worry.

In Philippians 4:6-7, Paul writes,

Do not be anxious about anything, but in every situation, by prayer and petition, with thanksgiving, present your requests to God. And the peace of God, which transcends all understanding, will guard your hearts and your minds in Christ Jesus.

"Do not be anxious about anything." Easier said than done. And not something you necessarily want to hear when you're wound up in worry. But God is offering you another way: A gentler way. A kinder way. A way that leads to peace. When you find yourself beginning to meditate in the wrong direction, he invites you to redirect your thoughts and fears to him. Turn your inner monologue into an open dialogue with God. Let him in by bringing your worry into the light. The simplest way to do it is to just tell him what you're worrying about in that moment, however big or small it may be.

"God, I'm worried about where our kids are going to go
   to school."
"God, I'm stressed about my to-do list at work today."
"God, I am tied up in knots over the state of our nation
   right now."
"God, I'm worried sick over my mom being in the
   hospital right now."

Name what's going on in your heart before it stakes its claim on your heart. And then as you do, transform your anxiousness into asking.

"God, will you give us the wisdom to know what to do
   with our kids' schooling? Please help us remember
   that you've taken care of them every day of their lives."
"God, will you remind me that the burden is light and

help me to work hard within my human limitations
today?"

"God, I pray for our leaders, that they will seek and find
your wisdom today. And will you show me how I
can shine a little of the light of your love in my world
today?"

"God, will you protect and heal my mom? Will you
calm her fears and mine? Will you guide the doctors
and all those who are caring for her today?"

And then in the next breath, turn your worry into worship. Philippians 4 calls this "thanksgiving." We've discussed
it at length earlier in the book, but for the sake of this conversation, it can look something like this:

"God, thank you that you are in control. I'm so grateful
that you hold not only *the* future but also *my kids'*
futures in your hands."

"God, thank you for this job. Thank you for providing
for me through it. And thank you for telling me that
I already have all I need for life and godliness. I'm so
glad to know you are with me every moment I spend
at work."

"God, thank you for your Kingdom, which is greater
than any nation. Thank you that I have a perspective
far greater than politics and that whatever comes my
way, you are never surprised and always in control."

"God, thank you for my mom. Thank you for all the

ways that she's cared for me. And thank you that in this season, you're inviting me to care for her."

You can make a shift in a moment. You can change the direction of your attention back to God. You can go from heavy to light. From beaten down to filled up. From worry to worship. And as you do, God promises that he will give you something far greater in exchange: He will give you peace. Peace to guide you. Peace to guard you. Peace to cover you. Peace to carry you. He'll replace the hours wasted in worry with greater purpose and peace.

WHAT, ME WORRY?

When I was growing up, a popular (albeit often inappropriate) magazine for kids was *MAD Magazine*. Let me try that again for some of this book's younger readers: Many years ago, there were things called magazines. They were like Book Lites, only printed on paper that was stapled together. Articles were in between the ads. (Sort of like if someone printed your favorite website. Anyway.) One of those magazines was *MAD Magazine*. It had a comical, satirical take on politics, pop culture, and current events. *MAD Magazine* had a mascot. His name was Alfred E. Neuman, and he had a famous slogan. His slogan, which was printed in every edition, was simply this: "What, Me Worry?" It embodied Neuman's careless and clueless approach to life. Nothing got him riled. Nothing got him roused.

It's easy to think that the solution to whatever you worry

about is to just stop worrying. Like Alfred E. Neuman, just go through life pushing down or pushing away whatever fear arises. But this would be both irresponsible and unsustainable. No matter how big or small, your fears and worries cannot be ignored; they must be transformed. They need to be turned *to* God and turned *into* something else. Something better. Something greater.

Years ago, on a ten-day trip to the Middle East, I was struck by the calls to prayer that occurred no matter what city I was in. Five times every day, a bell would ring or a loudspeaker would blare for all to hear that it was time to stop what you were doing, no matter what it was, and pray. I was there to film a video Bible study. Inevitably, our crew would be setting up or in the middle of a shot when bells would toll or a loudspeaker would go off. There are far too many outtakes to count of me trying to make a powerful point about God—only to get cut off right in the middle of a sentence. The audacity! Couldn't the entire city just wait a moment for me to get a clean take?!? There I was trying to teach people about God, and I was being taught an invaluable lesson about prayer.

What if you viewed your worry like those bells? Like a loudspeaker reminding you that it's time to pray, to transform your worry into a way of connecting with God? Let worry draw your attention in the direction of God. When you feel it rising, when you start grinding your teeth, when you start biting your nails, when your stomach starts to knot—all of these symptoms are invitations to do what Jesus taught you. To remind you that worry is a treadmill that leads you nowhere but leaves you exhausted in the end. To remind you how much God cares for you. To name your worries out loud to God, bringing them to the light. Invite him in. Allow him to speak into your worry. As you do—as you make this your prayer practice—see if he doesn't give you something you couldn't seem to rustle up on your own: the peace he promises to give if you are willing to turn your meditation toward him.

PRACTICE

This week, as you find yourself worrying about this or that (which you—and I—will most assuredly do), practice this transformational shift: Name your worries out loud to God anytime and every time they come up. Do it in the moment. Let your worry be an invitation to change the direction of your meditation. In that moment, choose to shift your thoughts to God.

"God, I'm worried about . . ."
"God, will you help me . . ."
"God, thank you that you are . . ."

This simple practice, done in real time, will have a powerful, transformational effect on your heart and mind. Pay attention to your heartbeat slowing, your breaths deepening, your tension easing. Look for the immediate physical effects of this spiritual practice. Each one is a gift from God and a reminder that he is with you and is giving you the peace he promises. The peace you need. The peace only he can give.

PRAYER

Gracious God,
you are surprisingly unsurprised.
You are not worried about a thing.
Thank you for inviting me to do the same.
Help me to trust you.
Help me to rest in your relentless love.
Help me to see that every little worry is an
invitation to change the direction of my attention.
Help me to transform my worry into worship.
And give me the peace that you promise,
the peace that settles this anxious, wayward,
and worry-bound heart.
The peace that guides and guards.
The peace that I need.
The peace that only you can give.

(deep breath)

Amen.

5

WHEN I AM GRIPPED BY GRIEF

If we do not transform our pain,
we will most assuredly transmit it.

RICHARD ROHR

Let me say this before I say anything else. If you are in a season of grief and loss, nothing I can say will take away the pain you are experiencing. Nothing. Nor would I want to do that. Not because I want you to suffer in sadness, but because as you already or will one day know, few things in life transform you more than grief. No one wants to hear this when they are grieving. No one.

I will never forget the words my wife said while we were in the hospital after saying good-bye to her father, Bill, who had died unexpectedly while running a race with Jeanne's brother, Eddie. In between uncontrollable sobs, she said, "I know that one day, God will use this. I know that I will

never be the same. But right now, I just want my dad back."
She was right. She is not the same. That tragic loss forever
changed her. She does not view life or death or God or family
or friends the same. It transformed her. That's what grief can
do—if you let it.

Grief is the gift that nobody wants. It comes to us wrapped
in sandpaper with a barbwire bow. The mystery of what's
inside the gift of grief has the power to grow your faith or to
blow it up. I have borne witness to both. Whether you allow
grief to open your heart to God or to cause you to turn your
back on him, the result is the same: You will not be the same.

C. S. Lewis wrote out of his own personal loss that "in
grief nothing 'stays put.'"[1] Whether you are grieving the loss
of someone you love, the death of a dream, or the state of
our nation, when you fully give your-
self over to grief, when you really do
the work that grief requires, you come
out as someone different on the other
side. Someone deeper. Someone more
soulful. Through loss, you find some-
thing new in yourself—something that simply would not be
true had you not chosen to grieve.

> Grief is a gift wrapped
> in sandpaper with a
> barbwire bow.

The question then, as it relates to this book, is this: Will
you grieve with God? Will you invite God in rather than
shut him out? Will you trust him to guide you through this
"valley of the shadow of death" (Psalm 23:4, ESV)? If your
answer is yes, then you are ready to enter the deeper journey.
You are ready to walk the often narrow, ever-winding path

of transformation that is only available to those willing to grieve, to those who are willing to walk with rather than away from God.

I have no words that can take away your grief, but I would like to offer a way to transform your grief. A way of praying through your grief that allows for hope and heartache to cohabitate. A way of praying that is both raw and redemptive.

THE UNINVITED JOURNEY

Grief comes to us all, regardless of whether it's invited. And let's be honest: Who invites grief anyway? Grief first came to me when I was eight years old, when I lost Maynard. I loved Maynard. We were best friends. He lived with me for a season. Maynard was my parakeet. And what a good parakeet he was! He would sit on my finger or rest on my shoulder, and he only tried to fly away twice. He was the first pet that I was truly responsible for. He stayed in my room in a cage right by the window (in hindsight, I suppose this was sort of cruel). All day, he would watch out the window as birds of all kinds would fly by and mock him with their freedom. But Maynard was (mostly) loyal, nonetheless.

One Sunday morning, I left for church, leaving the window open for Maynard to connect with his bird brethren while I was gone. What I didn't know was that we'd had our last time together. You see, during this season, our area was facing a crisis: an infestation of Mediterranean fruit flies had broken out in Northern California. To treat this threat, helicopters were regularly flying by, spraying malathion (*see*: kill). Because of the strength of this industrial pesticide, residents were encouraged to keep their windows closed during these area-wide sprayings. I didn't get that memo. Neither did Maynard. When I came home from church, I found Maynard at the bottom of his cage, "resting," as my sister tried to convince me. I was heartbroken. Inconsolable. How could a good God allow this to happen? We buried Maynard that afternoon, and I spent the next seven days sitting shiva. Within a year, I had moved on from a parakeet to tropical fish—all of which eventually died as well.

The point is that grief finds you. Sooner for some than for others. More for some than for others. But eventually, it finds us all, which is why it's so important that you know what to do when grief works its way to you. As a pastor, I've had to perform more funerals than I care to count. One funeral is more than enough. The very first funeral I performed was when I was twenty-eight years old. It was for a man I had never met. His wife had been coming to our church and loved listening to me preach. She would bring her three- and five-year-old sons with her regularly, but her husband rarely came. He had been in and out of rehab, suffering from a serious drug addiction that had cost him several jobs and had forced them to move more than once. He had finally gotten back on his feet and was out of rehab and working a night shift when he relapsed. He overdosed and was gone before anyone even knew or had a chance to say good-bye. As I stood there in that funeral home with only a handful of people in attendance, doing my best to offer words of comfort and hope to a wife and mother who had been to hell and back multiple times, I knew this woman and her boys would never be the same.

I have led funerals for friends, family members, and people I barely knew. It doesn't matter whose funeral it is, what the cause of death is, or whether people saw it coming, one thing remains the same: Grief places a fork in the middle of the road that your life was on. Which way you go is entirely up to you. I've seen people's lives take all kinds of routes through and around grief. Some people embrace it. Some people avoid it. Some people stay stuck in it. But one thing is for certain: You cannot continue to go the way you were going. The road of the life that you once knew is no longer available to you. I wish it weren't so. But this is how grief works. It reroutes and redirects. Lewis was right—nothing stays put.

If you're willing to walk grief's new path (albeit a longer and lonelier path than we would ever want), there is comfort in knowing that you don't have to walk it alone. God wants to walk with you, to carry you through the parts of the valley of the shadow of death where your will is waning and hope seems all but lost. He wants to lead you to new places where that old road simply could not lead you—but you must be willing to walk, work, and pray your way through grief to get there.

> Grief places a fork in the middle of the road that your life was on.

JOB'S JOB

There are many stories of grief and loss throughout the Bible. Within the first few pages, there is the murder of Adam and Eve's son, Abel, by his own brother (Genesis 4:1-16). Naomi grieves the loss of her husband and two sons and being left "alone" (Ruth 1:3-21). David grieves the rebellion of his son Absalom (and his untimely death before they could reconcile; 2 Samuel 18). There's even a whole book in the Bible, Lamentations, that teaches us the importance of recognizing and honoring what has been lost. But no story in the entire Bible is more associated with grief and loss than that of Job.

If you know the story, you know that Job had it all. He is described as the wealthiest person in the East. He was a man of importance and influence. His land and livestock were limitless. Picture Jeff Bezos and all his endless Amazon boxes. On top of that, the Bible says that Job was a man of integrity. His vast wealth and influence hadn't corrupted his character as it so often and so easily does. He and his family prospered. All was right and well in Job's world (Job 1:1-3).

And *that* is what you call foreshadowing! It makes for a great start to a story, because you know that things aren't going to stay this way. What ends up happening is that Satan has a conversation with God behind the curtain of creation. I'm not sure how this meeting got onto God's calendar, but nevertheless, they met. Apparently, Satan knew about Job—his wealth, his accomplishments, his integrity, and his love for God. And Satan wanted to see what would happen if Job lost it all. Would he still love God? God, knowing Job's character, allowed this to happen, with only one condition: Satan was not allowed to kill Job. Everything else was fair game (Job 1:6-12). This setup alone is difficult to wrap our heads around, theologically speaking, but this is the context we are given. And the story only gets worse from there.

Satan wasted no time. He never does. Job lost all his wealth. His servants. His livestock. All ten of his children died. (I can barely comprehend *having* ten children, let alone losing them all!) Then he was struck with an intense illness that would eventually make him a social outcast (Job 1:13-22; 2:7-13; 16:10; 19:13-19). Loss after loss. Grief after grief. All in rapid succession. This cannot be brushed over lightly. When you read it like a news report rather than a fairy tale, the weight of Job's losses becomes unbearable. Despite having experienced our own levels of losses, it is hard for us to fathom this level of human pain and suffering. All he had left was his wife and his faith.

Job was once a man of honor; now he was humbled and broken down. He had come to the end of himself. Job 1:20 says that after he lost his servants, livestock, and children, "Job got up and tore his robe and shaved his head."

Why did Job tear his robe and shave his head? First, this was part of a Jewish practice of mourning. It was the beginning of the grieving process known as "shiva." Shiva is a week of intense lamenting, grieving, and mourning. Grief does not end at the end of the week, but for that week, it is honored and welcomed. Job was clearly in shock. Just about everything he had and loved was stripped from him. Everything he held dear was gone—not just his resources but also all ten of his children. Can you imagine that degree of loss? I've attended and performed several funerals for children. Grieving the loss of a child is a gut-wrenching form of grief. Death and loss are already more than enough to bear, but when it's a child, it can feel like there isn't a space big enough to hold that kind of pain.

Job's response to the fork in the road placed by loss and grief is worth paying attention to. The Bible says that Job "fell to the ground in *worship*" (Job 1:20, emphasis added), saying,

> Naked I came from my mother's womb,
>   and naked I will depart.
> The LORD gave and the LORD has taken away;
>   may the name of the LORD be praised.
> JOB 1:21

Then it adds,

> In all this, Job did not sin by charging God with wrongdoing.
> JOB 1:22

Job literally fell. This crushing and pressing loss could no longer be sustained by his body. The loss was so immense. But what is worth noting is that when he fell to the ground, he worshiped. His worship took the same form of lament that we find in many of the psalms. It is one of the deepest, most honest forms of worship. Even as Job cried out from the depths of his being, "I have nothing. I came into this world with nothing, and now I have been stripped of everything I hold dear," Job acknowledged the mystery of God: that God gives *and* takes away. This is a profound insight to find in the dark tunnel of grief. God does not necessarily cause our losses, but God *allows* things and people to be taken away. Somehow, even as Job ran around the stages of grief (denial, anger, bargaining, depression, acceptance) in a matter of seconds, he still found the faith and fortitude to say, "May the name of the LORD be praised." Job didn't understand, but in his despair, he deepened his dependence on God.

The majority of the book of Job is a picture of how he sinks deeper and deeper into the soil of grief. In fact, in the next chapter, we see that the only person left in Job's family, his wife, was so undone by grief that at a particularly low point, she said to Job,

> Are you still maintaining your integrity? Curse God and die!
>
> JOB 2:9

(Thanks, dear. You always know *just* what to say!) But for her, it's all too much: The loss. The ache. The misery. The questions. The grief.

Job's reply is remarkable: "Shall we accept good from God, and not trouble?" (Job 2:10). Job got it. He knew that no matter what, grief finds us. We cannot experience this life and escape loss. He knew that even though everything he once loved and held dear—and the path he was once on—was no longer available to him, even though none of it made any sense, letting go of God in grief would mean sinking into a bottomless abyss. Job would lose his way through life unless he accepted that God *was* his way through this loss.

If you know the story, you probably remember that eventually Job's health was restored. His wealth and influence returned. He ended up with twice as much as he had before. More importantly, God blessed Job with ten more children (Job 42:10-13). This tragic and triumphant tale does have a happy (albeit hard-fought) ending. Job 42:12 says,

The LORD blessed the latter part of Job's life more than the former part.

The second half of his life—the part after his grief—was blessed. More blessed than the first part. More blessed than that first path. There is life and blessing on the other side of grief. It may not be what you thought, or even what you wanted, but there is blessing nonetheless.

Job's life is a picture of grief and grace. We will have moments of delight and moments of despair. Our hearts will expand with pure bliss, and they will also crack open and break in such a way that we'll wonder if we'll ever be able to carry on. It is never one or the other. It is always eventually both.

Job honored the loss in his life. He didn't deny or dismiss it. He accepted it for what it was, as hard as it was. And more importantly, he refused to lose God in his loss. He found a way to pray and worship though his throat was sore from wailing and his heart was broken from grieving. He held out for and held on to hope. And although he couldn't see what would come next, he never lost sight of God. He was honest with God and with his grief. During the darkest season of his life, Job's job was to hold on to God however he could. To walk through grief *with* God. And in the process, to be utterly transformed because of it. That is your job too.

UNDERWATER BEACH BALLS

Determination to pray through your grief is how you don't lose your grip on God. Whatever your grief may be—whether it's the loss of someone you love, the death of a dream, the end of a season, or a turn in the story that you didn't see coming—all change is loss. And all loss changes things. No matter how big or how small it may seem, if something has been lost, it needs to be grieved.

When grief isn't honored and given the time and space to do what only it can do, it becomes like a beach ball held underwater: It can't stay down forever. Eventually, it will come up. And it usually comes up sideways. Undealt-with or unprocessed grief can come out as deep, sustained depression. Unattended grief can manifest as fear. It can take the form of a fear of commitment. A fear to love again. A fear to trust. A fear to dream.

> **All change is loss. And all loss changes things.**

Grief that is not taken to God can end up being taken out on others—and/or yourself. I have a friend who lost his dad at a relatively young age. It was a massive loss, to say the least. Over the years, I have watched his grief take the form of detachment. This once outgoing, life-of-the party friend has largely pulled away from friends. He's been in a drift with his calling, and the light that burned so brightly from his life has gotten lost in the shadow of grief.

Praying your way through your grief, however difficult or daunting it may seem, allows you to bring the beach ball of your soul back to the surface in time. It can become your first form of processing what has been lost. Counselors, recovery groups, and soul-level friends are vital to your healing process. They all play a part. But prayer is a way for you to process your grief in real time, at any time. It's also a way to bring your whole (albeit broken) heart to God, one piece at a time, and to allow him to heal, restore, and transform you over the fullness of time. As challenging as prayer may be in the face of your grief, it is a far better way through grief than going sideways.

START WITH WHAT IS

One of the most important things you can do with God is acknowledge what has been lost. Again, like so much in prayer, this is more for you than it is for God. But it's important that you bring it all to God. This is what we see David do throughout so many of the psalms: He unapologetically brings his pain and his loss and his grief to God. He doesn't hold back. These are often our most honest prayers—and usually our simplest ones. "God, I am heartbroken." "God, I am so angry." "God, I feel so lonely." "God, I feel empty."

So much of loss and grief is a mystery. Most of our questions go unanswered this side of heaven. But how you are feeling— the state of your heart and soul—doesn't need to be an enigma; it needs to be expressed. It doesn't need to be sanitized. It just needs to be spoken, even if only in a few words. When you are faithful to those words, more will eventually come. Perhaps one of the most important prayers you can pray when grief comes your way is to simply say, "God, I am _____." He can handle it. He will know what to do with it. He will be with you as you say it. I agree with Dr. Henry Cloud:

> Grief is accepting the reality of what is. That is grief's job and purpose—to allow us to come to terms with the way things really are, so that we can move on. Grief is a gift of God.[2]

So . . . are you willing to start with what is?

ASKING BETTER QUESTIONS

Often when grief comes, the first question I have is *Why?* Why did this have to happen? Why now? Why them? Why me? It's about as human a response as possible. Something in our heads tells our hearts that having the answers we want will give us the comfort we need. The only problem is that we rarely get the answers we want, and when we do, they are rarely as comforting as we had hoped they would be.

Perhaps a better question to take to God in prayer is *What?* or *Who?*

Whom have I lost?

What is it about them that I love and miss most?

What did I love about what was before this fork in the road?

What am I saying good-bye to?

What or whom might I become because of this change that seems to have changed everything?

Those questions *have* answers. Those answers lead you to a deeper connection to what is and the God who is there. They are the guardrails that can guide you on this new path. And they offer glimpses of what God is up to and how he is transforming this loss into growth. Listening to God for the answers to those questions has the potential to bring not only comfort but also context. That helps give grief a place. The goal of praying through grief is not to eliminate sadness and loss but to give it its proper place. You will always carry this grief with you, but it doesn't have to drive you. God created you with the capacity to carry grief. Your soul can bear it. What prayer does in these dark and difficult days is help grief find its place—and ultimately, it helps you find your way.

BUT YOU PROMISED

When your whole world has been turned upside down, it's important to hold on to what you know. To what is true.

To what was true before and what is true still. Praying the promises of God is a powerful way to keep your feet on the ground and your eyes toward heaven as you walk through a season of grief. You can pray promises that God has already made to you, promises that he has yet to break. Promises like

The LORD himself goes before you and will be with you; he will never leave you nor forsake you. Do not be afraid; do not be discouraged.

DEUTERONOMY 31:8

Even though I walk
    through the darkest valley,
I will fear no evil,
    for you are with me;
your rod and your staff,
    they comfort me.

PSALM 23:4

God is our refuge and strength,
    an ever-present help in trouble.

PSALM 46:1

No one is cast off
    by the Lord forever.
Though he brings grief, he will show compassion,
    so great is his unfailing love.

LAMENTATIONS 3:31-32

[Jesus said,] "Blessed are those who mourn,
for they will be comforted."

MATTHEW 5:4

[Jesus said,] "Peace I leave with you; my peace I give to
you. Not as the world gives do I give to you. Let not
your hearts be troubled, neither let them be afraid."

JOHN 14:27, ESV

Rather than turning your back on God, turn your heart to
his promises. Hold him to his Word. Remind him of what he
already knows and claim these promises as your own.

BORROWING FAITH

When my friend Jeremiah died several years ago, I didn't know
if I had enough faith to make it through my grief, let alone
help lead others through. I was heartbroken. We all were. As I
mentioned in the introduction of this book (I'm not offended
if you skipped that part), Jeremiah had been one of the first
worship leaders in our church. He had taught us to worship
God. So it was fitting that at his celebration service, with people
pouring out into the lobby and all the way to the front door, we
worshiped. We worshiped for hours! We worshiped hard. With
hearts broken and hands raised, we worshiped. As I stood in the
front of our church with tears flowing down my face, I found
myself only able to sing a few songs. It's not that I didn't know
the words—it's that I found them hard to authentically own. I
knew that I believed in God; I just wasn't sure if I believed the

words to these songs. So I borrowed the faith of those around me. I stopped singing and let others sing for me. I listened to the words they sang. I let them speak to me. I suppose much of the time, worship is my act of profession. It's my professing what I believe to be true about God. But sometimes, worship is my confession. It's my admitting that I need to let these truths speak to me more than I need to speak them in that moment; it's that there is faith enough to borrow when mine is low.

Having walked with friends through their grief, I am always amazed when they show up at church during the lowest seasons of their life. Not because they have anything to give, necessarily, but because they desperately need to receive. What they so often need is to borrow the faith of others. To be held. To be carried. To be buoyed up by others in a seemingly endless torrent of grief.

If you find yourself in a season of grief, perhaps one of the best things you can do is just that: borrow others' faith. Just show up and feel no pressure to speak or offer anything. Perhaps the bravest thing you can do is put yourself in a place where you know God is (which is anywhere and everywhere) and where there are people of God who are more than willing to let you borrow some of their faith.

A GRACE DISGUISED

I remember hearing the story of Jerry Sittser years ago. He and his wife, Linda, married young and spent the first years of their marriage trying to start a family. But they just couldn't seem to get pregnant. Finally, after years of trying, it worked.

Like . . . *really* worked! They had four kids in six years! All was well. About two years after their youngest was born, they were hit by a drunk driver while Jerry was driving the family car. In that accident, he lost his wife, a daughter, and his mother, who happened to be with them. Three generations of women gone. Jerry became a single dad in an instant, left to raise his remaining three children (ages two, six, and eight) alone. What began for him that day was a journey of grief that he is still travelling thirty-some years later. Jerry was and is a follower of Jesus and a professor at a Christian university. He knew all the verses and passages that speak to God's heart for us when we are in grief. But rather than teaching a lesson on the subject, he was now the student, learning how to hold on to God when everything else was turned upside down.

Years later, Sittser wrote an invaluable field guide for grief, a book called *A Grace Disguised*. Today it stands as one of the single greatest works on grief ever written—right up there with C. S. Lewis's *A Grief Observed*. I've read and reread Sittser's book several times. It helped me hold on to God in seasons when grief had its grip on me. I remember coming across this glimmer of hope and healing while grieving the loss of my father-in-law, Bill. Sittser writes about what God can do when we choose to walk with him through our seasons of grief and loss, no matter how big or small we perceive them to be:

It is therefore not true that we become less through loss—unless we allow the loss to make us less, grinding our soul down until there is nothing left but an external self entirely under the control of circumstances. Loss can also make us more. In the darkness we can still find the light. In death we can also find life. It depends on the choices we make.[3]

You do not have a choice in whether grief will find you. It will. The choice you *do* have is how you respond. Whether you seek God or abandon him. Whether you show up to pray even if you don't have anything to say. Whether you allow the gift of grief to become a transforming work of grace in your life. My prayer for you is that you do—that you pray your way through grief, not around it—and that on the other side, you see that the prayers sown in the soil of grief can reap a harvest of transformation that can change the rest of your life.

COME AS YOU ARE

At just about every funeral I unfortunately find myself at, I am struck with the thought, *I don't know how people do this without God.* Grief is already hard enough *with* God. But the thought of walking through the valley of the shadow of death *without* God? I don't know how people do it.

It is true that I have seen grief, in its many faces and forms, lead people away from God. The anger, the unanswered questions, the pain and loss can all feel like too much. I've seen broken hearts lead to clinched fists. I've seen unprocessed grief work its way out through addiction, anxiety, unhealthy anger, and all sorts of other expressions. I've seen people fight grief only to lose the fight before the final round. Grief takes all that you've got and then some. So why wouldn't you take what God has to offer? Take the grace and hope and comfort and growth that he promises? Take his presence and his power to make it through another day? Take the faith of others and borrow it for as long as you need it?

Take all that you need by taking your grief to God in prayer. He can handle it. Remember, he is a Father who knows the pain of losing a child. He knows what you're going through and welcomes you to come as you are. To weep. To vent. To sit in silence. He invites you to come, he promises to be with you, and he promises to stay with you. And he promises that if you do, you will never be the same.

PRACTICE

If you are in a season of grief, I invite you to practice the Prayer of What Is. Set aside a time (or several times) every day when you check in with God. The check-in is simply this: Answer the question, *What's here now?* What are you feeling in the moment? Our friend Jeanne Malnati uses the acronym SASHET to check in. It stands for

Sad
Angry
Scared
Happy
Excited
Tender

(Yes, I know that it's not how you spell the word *sachet*, but go with it.)

Your prayer can be as simple as "God, I feel angry" or "God, I feel tender" or "God, I feel happy." That's it. If you want to expand, feel free. If not, that's okay. The point is for you to live in real time with your emotions and bring them to God in any given moment.

By doing so, you are simultaneously anchoring yourself to the here and now and to a hope beyond. By inviting God in, you are acknowledging that while this is what you are feeling in this moment, this is not all that there is. And the more and more you do, the more and more you begin to see and know that there is more. There is more than grief. More than sadness. More than loss. Simply by acknowledging and welcoming God in, you are reminding yourself that there is more.

PRAYER

God of all comfort,
comfort me in this loss.
Hold me and remind me that you will never let me go.

Help me to welcome the gift of grief.
I do not want it, but I welcome it.
Help me to not make it any bigger or smaller than it is.
Help me to walk all the way through it.

Forgive me for thinking I could get through life without
this—and without you.
Forgive those who try to tell me and sell me that it will
be okay.
Forgive me for wanting to punch them.

Remind me that it will not only be okay one day but that
it is also okay right here and right now, with you.
I am okay in your presence.
Help me to stay in your presence and connected to you.

I am counting on you to make good on your promises.
I need you to.

Thank you for the work that you are already doing in me
as I pray this prayer.
I will do what only I can do.
Now, God, I pray:
Do what only you can do in all the places and ways that
I am undone.

Amen.

6

WHEN I NEED DIRECTION

*I pray that I am never so foolishly naive or roguishly pompous
to think that I can be the captain of my own ship, for if God
is not at the helm my ship will soon be at the bottom.*

CRAIG D. LOUNSBROUGH

We live in a beautiful world. We live in a world where you can order all your groceries online and have them delivered to your house within an hour. We live in a world where you can do a video call with your kids—on a plane—for only forty-five dollars an hour for Wi-Fi. We live in a world where a drone will deliver new printer cartridges to your front door. But the most amazing technological advancement in the last fifteen years is the advent of GPS on your phone. Gone are the days of asking strangers for directions. Gone are the days of origami maps that require unfolding and folding while driving. Gone are the days of poster-size Rand McNally road atlases that double as windshield visors. Gone are the days of getting lost.

Many years ago, before the dawn of Google Maps, Jeanne and I drove from Chicago to California in the middle of winter in a 1988 Honda Prelude. We spent a day or so mapping out our journey. We kept multiple maps tucked in the tiny glove box of that tiny car. When our radiator cracked somewhere in the middle of Oklahoma, we had to pull over to find a pay phone and use a phone book to find a local mechanic in a town we'd never been to before. When we hit a blizzard in New Mexico, we had to reroute in real time using a comically sized atlas. We made it, but not without having to stop multiple times to ask for directions. But more importantly than that, we made it through as a couple and are still here to tell the story!

As I think back to that trip, I can't help but feel like we were some sort of settlers, braving off into a new world that no Google Street View car had ever tread before. Asking for directions while driving is a thing of the past. No one does it anymore. But that doesn't mean that we don't need direction. That doesn't mean that we don't ask for direction from God and from others when we hit roadblocks in life or forks in our proverbial roads. As long as big life decisions need to be made, we will need direction.

A COUPLE MILLION DECISIONS

Unfortunately, there is no GPS for life's biggest decisions. Try as we might, we simply cannot map out our lives. In his loving mercy, God invites us into his mystery by keeping our future hidden from us, which often leaves us needing direction and helps us to admit that we don't always know what to do or where to go.

This brings us to a fundamental—and potentially formational—human dilemma: What do you do when you don't know what to do? How do you make difficult decisions when you feel like you don't have all the data? How do you move forward when the next step isn't clear? How do you get to the intersection of faith and wisdom?

> In his loving mercy, God invites us into his mystery by keeping our future hidden from us.

If only there were Google Maps for life's biggest decisions. It would make life so much easier!

Me: Google, should I take this job in Cleveland?
Google: The current temperature in Cleveland is -7 degrees. Also, it's Cleveland, sooo . . .

Me: Google, should I finally ask her to marry me?
Google: Would you like me to show you your relationship history? I believe the data speaks for itself. The statistical odds of you finding someone else this good for you are 3,720 to 1.

Me: Google, should we skip going home for Christmas this year and seeing the in-laws?
Google: Calculating a route with the least amount of family drama . . . still calculating . . . still calculating . . .

Your life is filled with daily decisions. Some are big; some are small. But it's full nonetheless. Experts estimate that the average person makes seventy conscious decisions a day. Seventy conscious decisions! A conscious decision is a decision that requires your full attention in the present moment. These are bigger than just whether to go right or left or wear brown shoes or black. They are the kinds of decisions like

"Should I cover my tail with my boss or just own my mistake?"

"Should I stay and have another drink or call it a night?"

"Should I tell this person how I really feel or let it slide?"

And you make seventy of these conscious decisions a day. That's approximately 25,500 conscious decisions a year. Added up over seventy-five years, that's approximately 1,916,250 conscious decisions!

Over the course of your lifetime, you will make roughly two million conscious decisions. You will need direction some two million times in your life! Perhaps this is why Albert Camus famously said that "life is a sum of all your choices."[1]

Your decisions—especially the big and difficult ones—will one day tell the story of your life. Who you marry, where you live, which career you pursue, what you do with your resources, how you respond to life's challenges . . . all of it matters—not only for today but also for tomorrow. And not only for you but for others as well.

So often when faced with life's more significant decisions,

we end up getting stuck, stalling out, or circling around our lives without moving forward. Or worse yet, we end up just blindly picking a path and hoping that it all works out in the end. Some decisions may work out better than others, but the consequences of making big decisions without godly direction can be catastrophic.

What if there was a better way? A way of making big decisions *with* godly direction? What if you didn't come to God only as a last resort but instead started with God and the direction that he's already promised to give you?

Your decisions matter to God. No matter how big or small, they matter. They matter to God because *you* matter to God. And in his loving-kindness and overflowing wisdom, God offers you a way to pray through life's biggest decisions; to partner with him through prayer as you discern and decide.

AN INVITATION TO DIRECTION

Not surprisingly, the Bible has a lot to say about the decisions we make, the way we make them, and how we invite God into them. God is not unsure what to do when we lack clarity. Psalm 32:8 says,

> I will instruct you and teach you in the way
> you should go;
> I will counsel you with my loving eye on you.

The promise here is that God will instruct and direct you through your biggest decisions because he loves you. You may feel lost, but you are never lost to God. And that's not all. Isaiah 30:21 reminds us,

> Whether you turn to the right or to the left, your
> ears will hear a voice behind you, saying, "This is
> the way; walk in it."

I may want God to give me direction as quickly and clearly as possible, but God often guides through whispers and nudges. That's why Proverbs 3:5-6 invites us to

> Trust in the LORD with all your heart;
>   do not depend on your own understanding.
> Seek his will in all you do,
>   and he will show you which path to take. (NLT)

Again, we see God promising that when we come to him first, he will direct us. Pros and cons lists have their place, but so often my decisions are limited by my perception. I just can't see it all on my own. I need the wisdom and perspective of one greater than myself to see past myself. In Jeremiah 33:3, God promises as much:

> Call to Me and I will answer you, and I will tell you
> great and mighty things, which you do not know.
> (NASB)

God not only wants to inform you but also to transform you and grow in you greater dependence on him. James continues this theme when he says,

> If any of you lacks wisdom, you should ask God,
> who gives generously to all without finding fault,
> and it will be given to you.
> JAMES 1:5

In other words, when you don't know what to do, you know whom to ask. And the good news here is that God doesn't judge you when you don't know what to do. James does offer this caveat in James 1:6-8:

> But when you ask, you must believe and not doubt,
> because the one who doubts is like a wave of the
> sea, blown and tossed by the wind. That person
> should not expect to receive anything from the
> Lord. Such a person is double-minded and unstable
> in all they do.

Yeah, but James, tell us how you really feel! In no uncertain terms, James says that while we may be uncertain about what to do next, we don't need to be uncertain about God. In other words, we shouldn't view God's direction as one of many options.

A PROVERBIAL PATH

There are many stories, verses, and passages in the Bible that speak to our need for godly direction and God's willingness to offer it. But perhaps one of the most practical and prescriptive passages when it comes to seeking direction is found in the book of Proverbs. Whenever I have a big personal decision to make or when Jeanne and I have a big decision to make for our family, our future, or the church, the thing I most want to know is the destination. I just want to know where to go, but God is most interested in where I start. If you are praying for direction in your life, this is where God says to start: with wisdom. Proverbs 4:5-6 says,

> While we may be uncertain about what to do next, we don't need to be uncertain about God.

> Get wisdom, get understanding;
> do not forget my words or turn away from them.
> Do not forsake wisdom, and she will protect you;
> love her, and she will watch over you.

Seek godly wisdom, and you will find the guidance you seek. Regardless of what might be next, the best place to start is wisdom. Solomon, the wisest person who ever lived, also offers this helpful little gem:

The beginning of wisdom is this: Get wisdom.
Though it cost all you have, get understanding.
PROVERBS 4:7

Where does wisdom begin? By getting wisdom. Thanks, Solomon. If this king thing doesn't work out for you, you might want to consider a career as a fortune cookie writer.

Actually, his repetition is intentional. When seeking direction, nothing matters more than wisdom. God's wisdom is always free—but that doesn't mean it won't come at a cost to your pride, your plans, or your preferences.

Yet wisdom is well worth it. Listen to what wisdom will do for you over the course of your life:

When you walk, your steps will not be hampered;
when you run, you will not stumble.
Hold on to instruction, do not let it go;
guard it well, for it is your life.
PROVERBS 4:12-13

When you choose to walk in wisdom, you tend to get tripped up less. You can move forward in faith and freedom! You don't have to second-guess every decision. Listen to these words from God's heart for your life:

Pay attention to what I say;
turn your ear to my words.

Do not let them out of your sight,
    keep them within your heart;
for they are life to those who find them
    and health to one's whole body.
Above all else, guard your heart,
    for everything you do flows from it.
PROVERBS 4:20-23

Somehow along the way, our Western world made wisdom a thing of the head. We tend to equate wisdom with knowledge. But that couldn't be any further from the truth. Wisdom is a thing of the *heart*. It's not merely something you access when you need help making a decision—it's a way of living. It's like a real-time, whole-life GPS.

Solomon closes out his wisdom manifesto with this:

Give careful thought to the paths for your feet
    and be steadfast in all your ways.
Do not turn to the right or the left;
    keep your foot from evil.
PROVERBS 4:26-27

There will always be shortcuts. There are always detours that can derail your life. But when wisdom tells you the way to go, that's the way you should go. When wisdom gives you the next step, that's the step you should take, even if it seems like there's a quicker way of getting where you think you're going. There really are no exceptions to this principle. You are not the exception to the rule. We all have had our fair share of experiences when we knew what wisdom was and chose to go another way—when we chose to go our own way. Times when we broke from the huddle too early. Times we thought we knew better. We tend to store these stories in a shoebox labeled "Regrets." It just never works out like we thought it would when we walk outside of wisdom.

So what do you do when you don't know what to do? Get wisdom. Not opinion, not consensus. Not someone else's path or plans. Get wisdom—godly wisdom. Look for it. Listen to it. Do what it says. And you will find yourself in far better places than you could have gotten on your own.

So . . . how do you do it? I'm glad you asked!

THE CROCK-POT OF DISCERNMENT

When praying through a difficult or big decision, it's easy to only see the decision in front of you. You don't know what to do or what's best, and you want God to help you, preferably quickly and clearly. When Jeanne and I couldn't decide where to start Soul City Church, we just wanted God to tell us. We didn't need the exact address. The name of a city would have been fine. The answer to that question would set into motion many to-do lists in our life, so understandably we wanted God to move it to the top of *his* to-do list.

Before you go any further in your own decision-making, it's important to pay attention to *how* you want to make this decision. You are seeking God. That is a serious, spiritually significant thing! You are asking God to speak into your decisions and the direction of your life. Think about that for a moment. So many people make decisions without even thinking about what God thinks about them. Whether because they don't care what God thinks, don't know how to make decisions with God, or don't want God to slow things down or take them in an undesirable direction, people don't typically ask God for wisdom and guidance. But you are. That matters to God more than you know. And it's a far better way to live.

Praying through big decisions is a spiritual stew made of several ingredients: praying, reading the Bible, seeking godly wisdom, waiting, and moving forward in faith. Another word for this kind of prayer is *discernment*. Spiritual discernment is the process of bringing God in before moving forward. It's the decision to start—and stay—with God.

Recently, we had an addition to our family: something I honestly don't know how we lived without. We are now proud owners of a Crock-Pot. We are *big* fans of the Crock-Pot. There's nothing like loading the Crock-Pot with all the right things in the morning and then coming home to the aroma of a meal that's been cooking all day and is ready to be served. The Crock-Pot is the tortoise to the microwave's hare. "Oh, you can reheat cold pizza in two minutes? Isn't that cute. I'll just be over here making a meal for the whole family for the next eight hours. What's that you say? The middle of the pizza is still cold? Hmm . . . I wouldn't know anything about that."

Like a good Crock-Pot, spiritual discernment is the process of combining what God has already said with what God is currently saying and godly wisdom from others. Like a good stew, it requires letting the ingredients simmer until they're ready to serve your life and whatever decision you need to make or direction you need to take. Here's what that looks like.

WHAT HAS GOD SAID?

When you don't know what to do, ask yourself, *What has God already said? Does the Bible have anything to say about this? Has God already given me wisdom and direction that I can apply to my life in this decision?*

The Bible is essential to your transformation because God has said and is saying so much to you through it. And the more you are in it, the more it gets in you. The Bible is a wealth of wisdom that has stood the test of time.

Should I buy this car that's beyond my budget? Is it worth going into debt over? What has God said? Well, Proverbs 22:7 says that "the borrower is slave to the lender." Do I really want to be indebted to Tesla? (This is a real spiritual quandary for me. I mean, have you experienced their "Ludicrous Speed"?!?)

Should I move in with my boyfriend [or girlfriend] to save money—and to see if this relationship is going to work? What has God said? Well, Hebrews 13:4 says that "Marriage should be honored by all, and the marriage bed kept pure." In other words, there are some things that are far more important to save than money. This may be wisdom I don't want, but that doesn't mean there's not wisdom in it.

Should I fudge the truth at work to get ahead or to keep from getting in trouble? What has God said? Well, Proverbs 10:9 says that "whoever walks in integrity walks securely, but whoever takes crooked paths will be found out." There's real wisdom there. Yeah, but God, have you met my boss?

When you don't know what to do, the first and most important thing to do is to see what God has already said. Start there. Look for and listen to the wisdom that God has already given you. Let it guide and guard you as you encounter some of the two million decisions that you'll make in your life. Could it be that this is what King David meant when he said that "[God's] word is a lamp unto my feet, and a light unto my path" (Psalm 119:105, KJV)? Could it be that godly wisdom has the power and promise to direct your decisions, that it can tell you what to do when you don't know what to do? What might happen if you started with how God has already guided you?

So much of the direction that I come to God seeking has already been provided. But not always. Not every decision. With some decisions, for whatever reason, it's not necessarily clear what God has already said. What do you do then? Ask the next question.

WHAT IS GOD SAYING?

If you still don't know what to do, then ask yourself, *What is God saying?* Listening for and to God in real time is one of the main reasons we pray. And yet hearing from God remains one of the great mysteries of prayer. I'll admit that for a good part of my life, I was weary of people who said they "heard from God." Whether due to my own struggle with prayer or a generationally ingrained sense of skepticism, I just found it hard to believe that God actually "spoke" to people like he used to do in the Bible. Some of this skepticism came from an unnecessary abundance of 1980s books about how God had told certain pastors and authors when the world would end, or when America would be invaded by Russia, or why a certain presidential candidate would be elected. Despite their specificity of dates and convoluted use of Bible verses, none of the predictions that God had "told" them ever came to be.

Years ago, when I was working as the singles ministry director at another church, one of my team members talked about how someone she barely knew had "heard from God." At one of our big events, a man who had been around church for a little while came up to her and said, "God told me we're supposed to be together. I feel called to date you." Without missing a beat, she replied, "Well, if God called you, he clearly dialed the wrong number!"

Well played.

It's understandable if you are a little skeptical about God speaking to you. But that doesn't mean he doesn't. Several times in my life, God has spoken directly into decisions I was in the middle of making. He has yet to speak exactly how I want him to or to say exactly what I want to hear, but that doesn't mean he doesn't have something to say.

Sometimes God speaks directly to you. Just you and him.

Sometimes it's while you're praying; sometimes it's not. It can be as simple as a word or a phrase or even an image. Sometimes it comes in a dream or a vision. Sometimes it comes as a whisper. Other times it's more like a flying elbow drop from the upper rope (see "The Macho Man" Randy Savage from 1980s wrestling).

Years ago, when Jeanne and I were praying about a potential location for our church, we stood on the corner of an intersection in downtown Chicago on a blustery October morning. We got on our knees on the sidewalk and prayed that God would provide us with a physical space for our church to meet. We prayed specifically for the vacant warehouse space at that corner. When we finished praying, we got up and noticed a butterfly flying around us—not something you typically see in downtown Chicago . . . in October. It kept flying around us while we walked and talked and dreamed. We didn't think much of it until later that week.

Back in Atlanta, Jeanne's friend Lauren (who had been praying for us and our eventual church) told Jeanne that she'd had a vision while praying for us earlier that week. It was of a giant butterfly (stay with me) that Jeanne was riding (still with me?). Everywhere the butterfly went, things came to life. Lauren laughed while she told Jeanne about the vision, admitting that it all sounded a little crazy, but she felt responsible to share it with Jeanne. When Jeanne heard about this vision, she began crying. She told Lauren of the butterfly that wouldn't leave us alone just days earlier as we prayed over a building on a corner in downtown Chicago. That building became the home to Soul City Church, where we would eventually open a Transforming Center built on the belief that God brings new life to all people. In that building, in Jeanne's office, are paintings and pictures of butterflies. They serve as reminders of how God speaks and that he is always speaking, if we are willing to listen—and look.

It may seem a little weird or intimidating that you would *hear* from God, but nothing could be further from the truth. This is so much of what prayer is all about! It is talking and listening to God. Prayer is bringing your decisions to God and waiting for him to speak.

What about when it's not clear what God is saying to you or what he's already said in the Bible? That's when it's time to bring others into your prayer.

WHAT ARE GODLY PEOPLE SAYING?

If a decision or direction is still unclear after exploring what God has said and what God is saying, then ask yourself, *What are godly people saying?*

When you need to make a big decision, whom do you turn to? Whom do you invite in to help you decide? This is critically important. Once again, the good news is that you're better at this than you think! Think about the last time you were looking for a good restaurant, movie, or book. What did you do? You read the reviews! There's hardly any major purchase that we make without reading the reviews. We even read reviews for ninety-nine-cent apps! I recently read reviews for firewood. Yep, firewood. Do I go with oak, hickory, maple, cherry, or white birch? Which is best? And who has the best price and selection in the city? I spent thirty minutes researching and reading reviews—about firewood.

We let complete strangers speak into many of our daily decisions, so why wouldn't we seek godly wisdom for the life decisions that matter most? Why wouldn't you bring people in to help you see and hear what you can't?

Jeanne and I call this group of people our "wisdom well." It's where we draw godly wisdom from when we are seeking God's direction. It's made up of people we not only like but also want to *be* like—people whose lives are guided and guarded by godly wisdom.

For big decisions regarding our family, we seek out our friends and mentors Dick and Sibyl Towner and Marc and Jeanne Malnati. For big decisions regarding our church, we go to the church elders; our friends; fellow pastors Dave Davis, Daniel Hill, and Jon Peacock; and our former pastor, Andy Stanley. For big financial decisions, we seek out the godly wisdom of our friends Keith Cantrell and Andy Code.

We don't just ask for their opinions; we also ask them to pray with us and for us and to speak to us out of what *they* hear from God. We know they aren't going to tell us what we want to hear; they'll do their best to offer us wisdom from the heart of God. They may not even realize it, but they themselves are answers to our prayers. Since we were first married, Jeanne and I have prayed for God to bring godly, wise people into our lives to help us see what we can't see (and sometimes to hear what we can't seem to hear) from God.

This is what you can do when you don't know what to do; when you're praying for direction and the next step seems unclear; when you want your life to be led by God: Simply ask,

- What has God said?
- What is God saying?
- What are godly people saying?

You can't go back and change or erase bad decisions you've made. I have several that I wish I could, but I can't. No one can. But you *can* shape and direct your future by the choices that you make today. The decisions you make and the way you make those decisions make or break your future possibilities and potential realities. Your destiny is determined by your decisions. Your decisions tell the story of your life. And God is inviting you to invite *him* to be part of them. He has supplied you with an endless stream of eternal wisdom. It is yours for the asking—if you are willing to walk in his wisdom.

LIVING IN THE DIRECTION OF YOUR PRAYER

Have you ever filled out a college application? If so, do you remember how it felt? The stress. The hope. The endless essays. As a youth pastor in a former life, I wrote more than my fair share of reference letters for students who were willing to play the God card on their college applications. More power to them. They had their top three and top ten schools all lined up and picked out. Options on top of options. I envied them, because when I was their age, I employed a different strategy.

I only applied to one college. One. That's it. Cal State Hayward (now called Cal State East Bay). That was my entire elaborate plan. Apply to one school. No backup plan. No fallback options. Just one school. Thankfully, I got in (which is not saying much, because in those days, just about everyone who applied to Cal State Hayward got in). Shockingly, the school didn't have quite the same prestige as, say, Stanford or UC Berkeley (both of which were less than an hour's drive away). If you've ever been to Hayward, California, you'll understand why. I don't know why I only gave myself next to no options. Either I would go to Cal State Hayward or be one of the eleven applicants who didn't get accepted that year. Calling this a plan is being generous.

Your destiny is determined by your decisions.

It's easy to do the same thing when praying for direction: To ask God to guide you to a new job but not fill out any applications or set up any interviews. To ask God to bring a godly partner into your life but stay at home binge-watching *Friends*. To ask God to lead your marriage to a better place but stay committed to the same patterns that got you and your spouse into the rut you're currently in.

Praying for direction isn't passive. It's a partnership. It's your doing what only you can do while God does what only he can do. It's opening your life up for God to lead while you live in the direction of your prayer. It's aligning your life to the will and way of God (as much as you know it) while waiting for God to fill in the specifics.

If you've ever had to push a dead car, you already know this principle. It's much easier to turn the tires if the car is already moving, even if it's only at one mile per hour. The same is true of your life. God is a God of miracles. I have seen him make something out of nothing in my life. On more than one occasion, he has made a way when there was no way. But where I've seen God move the most in my life is when I'm living in the direction of my prayer, when I'm moving forward in faith and wisdom with as much as I know at the time, believing that God will give me the direction I need as I need it. And he can and will do the same for you.

Live in the direction of your prayer.

A DESTINATION GREATER THAN DIRECTION

Whatever you are seeking from God, whatever area of your life you need direction in, it is important not to forget that when you come to God, you get more than you ask for. What goal is greater than direction? *Connection.* Connection with God is far greater than any direction he may give you. This is, after all, the point of prayer.

Revered German pastor and theologian Dietrich Bonhoeffer knew this all too well. During the Second World War, Bonhoeffer spent the last two years of his life in German prisons. Bonhoeffer was arrested and ultimately executed by the gestapo, but he never stopped seeking God, even when it seemed he was out of options. In his book *Letters and Papers from Prison*, written in the final months of his life, Bonhoeffer said,

> May God in his mercy lead us through these times; but above all may he lead us to himself.[2]

This is such a profound and powerful way to pray. Ask God to lead. Ask God for direction. Ask God for wisdom. But always seek *him* first and above all else. Connection with God is the ultimate destination of the direction you seek. No matter what or where God may lead you to, he is always inviting you into deeper connection with him. God is far more concerned with your decision to be *with* him than he is with the decision that you need *from* him.

Ask. Seek. Knock. But in so doing, never lose sight of the one who answers. He is far more important than any answer you need. And your connection to and relationship with him will take you further than any decision you need an answer for or any direction you need revealed.

PRACTICE

What big decision is in front of you right now? Where do you need direction? Take a moment and get specific with it. Now ask yourself, *Am I willing to make this decision with God?*

Be honest. *Am I really willing to open my life, will, and plans to God? Am I really willing to seek his wisdom for this decision?* If the answer is yes, this is how you can begin to pray today. Ask yourself,

> *What has God already said?* Is there any wisdom God has already given that speaks—directly or indirectly—to this area of your life?
>
> *What is God saying?* Take time to be quiet. The greater the decision, the greater the listening. Don't be surprised if God doesn't lay out a life plan for you after two minutes of praying. Keep seeking. When you give God your attention, God gives you direction.
>
> *What are godly people saying?* Identify two or three people whom you want to be like and ask them to join you in prayer. Give them access to your life, and then give them time to listen with you. If you really want to go all in, don't just ask them to pray *for* you; ask them to pray *with* you. See how God might use them to speak into your life.

My genuine belief—based on the promises of God and evidence in my life—is that as you ask these questions, God will guide you. And my hope and prayer for you is that this will become not *a* way but *the* way that you make decisions and seek direction for your life, that this way of praying becomes what you do when you don't know what to do.

PRAYER

God of all wisdom,

speak.

Speak to me. Speak over me. Speak into me.

Guide and guard me like you have promised you will.

Help me to open my life to you,

to seek you first . . . and second . . . and third . . .
and always.

Thank you for how your Word speaks to me.

Thank you for how your Spirit speaks to me.

Thank you for how your people speak to me.

Help me to listen, to live in the direction I'm praying,
and to obey.

Thank you for your yeses and noes.

Your heres and theres.

Your nows and not yets.

Help me to see them all as gifts, as further evidence
of your goodness.

I trust you.

Amen.

7

WHEN I DON'T HEAR ANYTHING

Silence is God's first language.

JOHN OF THE CROSS

What makes prayer so powerfully faith forming and so potentially frustrating is the dynamic of dialogue. For most of the practices of the Christian faith, the responsibility lies on you. Communion is something that *you* receive. Baptism is something that *you* do (unless your parents did it for you as a baby, but let's be honest: If that's the case, you don't even remember it). Fasting is something that *you* choose (and no, forgetting to eat breakfast and lunch is not fasting; it's just poor planning). All these spiritual practices, and more, require *your* taking responsibility to initiate and to participate in the forming of your faith. Prayer, on the other hand, is a team effort. You *and* God, together, are involved in speaking *and* listening. It is dependent on the dynamic of dialogue. So what do you do when you are listening but it seems like God isn't speaking?

HELLO . . . IT'S ME

For years, the outgoing voice mail message on my phone went something like this: "Hello? . . . HELLO? . . . I'm sorry, I can barely hear you. Wait . . . there, I think I heard you. Can you speak up? . . . AI II II II I, just kidding. I'm not really here. Leave a message, and I'll get back to you."

I thought I was pretty clever. Apparently, not everyone felt the same. Many people would leave messages laughing, if not sounding slightly annoyed. My grandmother, Gen, however, was not amused. Her voice mails usually consisted of calling me a brat (or some other colorful name only she could get away with) and telling me how she fell for it every time, and that the next time she saw me, she was going to box my ears (I never really knew what that meant, but I knew she would do it!).

As funny as it was, that's precisely what prayer is like at times for many of us: Like we've dialed up God—hoping to hear from him, needing to hear from him—only to sense he isn't even there, like there's no one on the other end. After a while, it's easy to imagine that our prayers are nothing more than unanswered voice mails left for an otherwise preoccupied God.

Few things in this life are as defeating and deafening as the seeming silence of God. This is partly because we live in a world of constant noise, distraction, and instant inter-action. We live in a world of FaceTime and Facebook Live. We can be connected to people we've never met, from half-way around the world, whenever we want. The thought of God not showing up, or making us wait, or not giving us *what* we want, *when* we want it—well, that's unthinkable.

The great irony in our struggling with God's silence is that so often, silence is the very thing that *we* most often offer God. There have been far more times than I can count when I have been silent with God—or about God; times when God has spoken and I have chosen not to listen or respond. My hunch is that you have offered up your fair share of silence as well. Maybe you used to pray, and then you just . . . stopped. You went silent. And you don't really know how or when or why. Maybe you pray about certain things in your life but are silent with God about others, hoping that he won't ask or remember. We seem to have no problem with silence on our end, but when God doesn't speak to *us* how we want or when we want—when God is seemingly silent—it can be the breaking point of our faith.

Musician Andrew Peterson, who wrote the powerfully poignant song "The Silence of God," touches on pain from God's silence in his lyrics:

It's enough to drive a man crazy. . . .
Enough to make him wonder if he's ever been sane.
When . . . the heavens' only answer is the silence of God.[1]

If you have ever experienced the unsettling silence of God, you know what Peterson is getting at. You know what it's like to feel that God isn't there or maybe doesn't care.

What you may not know is that you are not the first to experience the silence of God. You are not the first person to face the vacuum left in the absence of God's voice. You are not the first, and you are not alone. Others have faced what you have faced or are facing right now. You may not have the answers you want from God, but at least you have company. Not only have others walked where you walk but someone also walks with you—even if you cannot currently hear his voice.

> **God may be quiet with you, but that doesn't mean that he's quit on you.**

The comforting, albeit confusing, truth is that God is with you. Even in the silence. Even in his silence. He may not be heard, but that doesn't mean he cannot be found. As hard as it may be to believe, silence is not the same as absence. God may be quiet with you, but that doesn't mean that he's quit on you.

HIDE-AND-SEEK

Our daughter, Gigi, used to love playing hide-and-seek. To be more specific, she loved to hide. When she was younger, just about every night when we went to tuck her in, we couldn't find her. I'm not kidding. Every night. She has been known to hide in her closet, under a pile of stuffed animals, behind doors—you name it. She once hid in our dirty-clothes hamper for ten minutes, waiting for us to stumble upon her. That's a commitment to her craft. She gets it from me: I've been hiding and scaring people my whole life. It's a tradition in my family. It's how we show love to one another. My wife, Jeanne, however, *hates* being scared. I learned this the hard way while we were dating. I hid in the back seat of her car for twenty minutes waiting for her one night. When I jumped up from behind to scare her, she punched me square in the chest. Lesson learned.

Have you ever felt as if God were playing a cosmic game of hide-and-seek with you? You call out for him. Nothing. Look in all the old familiar places. Nothing. If God is playing a game, it's not a very fun one. Desperation can turn to defeat in the presence of God's silence. But what if there's more? What if God isn't hiding *from* you but rather waiting *for* you? What if God isn't avoiding you but inviting you to join him in the silence? Even though you may not hear, that doesn't mean that God's not near. In fact, often it is in the silence that we find God is waiting for us—even while we wait for him. Could it be that silence is not something you need to run from but something you need to enter into? Could God have just as much for you in the silence as he does in the answer or provision you seek from him in prayer?

THE HEART OF HANNAH

Many characters throughout the Bible who came before you faced the silence of God and stood before its vast void.

Hannah is one of those people. She was a woman of faith who desperately desired to have a child but could not.

Perhaps you are familiar with Hannah's struggle or know someone who has gone through it. You know of the desperation and defeat that is born out of infertility, of the desire for God to hear your prayer and make a way. We have walked with several dear friends through the valley of the shadow of infertility. We have prayed with and for them. We have cried with them and grieved with them. And we have celebrated with those who, after years of sitting in the silence of God, were able to finally form a family. If you know anything about those kinds of prayers, then you know Hannah and her story.

The book of 1 Samuel tells us that Hannah was married to Elkanah, who was also married to another woman, Peninnah (things were . . . *different* back then).

The story starts with tension and a little bit of drama:

> [Elkanah] had two wives; one was called Hannah
> and the other Peninnah. Peninnah had children, but
> Hannah had none.
>
> 1 SAMUEL 1:2

This is so often how it is (aside from the part about having two wives). Whenever it's hard to find God, it's easy to find others who seem to have what we want. You may not be hearing from God, but you keep hearing about people who seemingly do—people whom God seems to like better than you.

This is what Peninnah represented to Hannah. But it gets

worse: Peninnah not only had what Hannah wanted but also gloated about it. She even mocked Hannah's pain:

> Because the LORD had closed Hannah's womb, her rival kept provoking her in order to irritate her. This went on year after year. Whenever Hannah went up to the house of the LORD, her rival provoked her till she wept and would not eat.
>
> 1 SAMUEL 1:6-7

Peninnah, who had children, was harassing Hannah, who did not. As if the suffering of being childless weren't enough, Peninnah was also there to rub it in!

Haven't you found there is *always* a "Peninnah" in your story? There is always someone who seems to make it their job to turn God's silence into your suffering. It can be indirect or unconscious, but there is something about their *having* that reminds you of your *not having*. Their *joy* reminds you of your *pain*.

And in the silence of God, it's easy to only hear the echoing taunts of others who try to convince you this silence is something that must be suffered. That God is mad at you, or worse: that God doesn't care about you. That you've done something wrong; or you're not doing something right; or you're not doing enough of this, that, or the other. But this couldn't be further from the truth, because

God's silence is not for the sake of your suffering.

what we see in the story of Hannah is that God's silence is not for the sake of your suffering.

Much like your story, Hannah's story isn't done just yet. We continue by reading about how her husband attempts to comfort her:

> Her husband Elkanah would say to her, "Hannah, why are you weeping? Why don't you eat? Why are you downhearted! Don't I mean more to you than ten sons?"
>
> 1 SAMUEL 1:8

This is a sort of sweet and well-intended gesture by Hannah's husband, Elkanah. He sees the depth of desire in her. He sees her pain. He knows of the taunts of Peninnah (you know, his *other* wife), and he tries to do something about it. Like husbands often do, he tries to fix it. Or more to the point, he tries to fix *her*. His solution is for her to downgrade her desire. He suggests she settle for something else to help dodge this deafening silence: *Rather than holding out for the thing you desire, why don't you settle in with what you already have?*

Just like there is always a Peninnah, there is always an Elkanah in your story: someone who loves you, who knows your pain or your longing to hear something from God and, in the face of the silence, offers you the opportunity to settle for something less than God's best. To settle for the guy you are with instead of holding out for a great, God-given partner. To settle for a comfortable life instead of living a courageous life of faith. To settle for something—anything— that drowns out the seeming silence of God. But what we learn from Hannah is that God's silence is not for the sake of your settling.

It is so easy to reach out for something else, something less, when you don't think you can hold out for God anymore, or when it feels like God is holding out on you. Settling is how your soul practices self-defense. Whether it's with the people we're dating or what we do with our money or having a difficult-but-needed conversation, we always look for the easiest way out. The path of least resistance. And the silence of God almost always gives us the inch that our souls turn into a mile.

God's silence is not for the sake of your settling.

But Hannah refuses to let silence succumb to settling. In a gut-wrenchingly honest prayer to God, Hannah commits to staying with God—even if he is silent. Rather than running from God, she chooses to stay with him until she hears something. Hannah, while weeping bitterly in deep anguish, enters into the silence.

Verse 16 gives us further insight into her strength in the midst of God's silence:

I have been praying here out of my great anguish and grief.

Rather than walking away, she steps in. She holds out and holds on to hope. She trusts God, letting him know exactly what she wants and that she isn't going anywhere. This isn't a demand she's placing on God; it's a display of faith in God. Hannah had no idea just how significant this prayer was or what God would do with it. Because wouldn't you know it . . .

> In the course of time Hannah became pregnant and gave birth to a son. She named him Samuel, saying, "Because I asked the LORD for him."
>
> 1 SAMUEL 1:20

Hannah gives us a powerful picture of what can happen when we stand in the face of God's seeming silence. Her story illustrates what can happen when we *pour out our hearts* rather than *pack up our bags*. The silence of God was not for the sake of suffering. Nor was it for the sake of settling. Rather, the silence of God is what gave Hannah's faith *strength*! It led her to leaning in. To greater faith. To listening for God alone over the taunts of Peninnah and the distractions of Elkanah. God's silence was for the sake of strengthening her faith. And the same is true for you and me.

What Hannah couldn't see at the time was that her years and years of tears were washing away all traces of superficial faith. This is often the unwelcome gift of God's silence: It strengthens and grows us in a way that always getting what we want—when we want it—never could! If you always got what you wanted, you would lose all relationship with God. He would be nothing more than a genie in a bottle, and you would become nothing more than a spoiled child living in a fairy-tale world. When you choose to stay with God in the silence, you grow. In the silence, you learn how to wait on God. You learn how to trust God. In the silence, you learn how faith is forged.

STUMBLING INTO SILENCE

Staying with God in the silence is more challenging than we know or care to admit. To be more specific, it is more challenging for *me* than almost any other form of prayer. I am the kind of person who is action oriented and distraction prone. I never won the silent game as a kid. For many years, silence

God's silence is for the sake of strengthening.

didn't seem like a spiritual discipline; it felt more like spiritual torture. My "silence muscle" was in atrophy for many years, and it still needs to be worked out on a regular basis.

A few years back, looking to develop this muscle and deepen my spiritual disciplines, I joined the Transforming Center, an intentional spiritual community led by Ruth Haley Barton that consists of people from all over the country who gather together every quarter over the course of two and a half years for spiritual retreats and community. Aside from teaching and participating in small groups, sharing meals, and having fixed hours of prayer, we spent *lots* of time in silence.

My first retreat was challenging, to put it mildly. Within hours of arriving, we were sent off for silent contemplation and weren't allowed to speak to another person for ten hours. The first hour, I tried. I really did. I read, wrote a little, and then felt an almost compulsive need to check my email. The second hour, I decided to channel my addiction to distraction into a walk. I walked the grounds. I spent time talking with God—and looking at my watch.

The next eight hours, I slept. Silence tends to come a lot easier for me when I'm asleep. To say that the first retreat was rough would be an understatement. But over the course of my time in the Transforming Center, I grew to love the silence.

Silence is a practice that I continue incorporating into my life today. It lets me come to God with my agenda, or my exhaustion, or my frustration, or my fears—and just sit, be still, and know that God is still God (Psalm 46:10). He is in control. He knows my every thought and need. He knows my struggle with silence. He knows what's best for me. And I know—or eventually come to know—that I am okay. I will be okay, even if I don't hear anything from God. Especially when I don't hear anything from God. He may be silent, but he is not absent. I may have to wait for what I want, but I am not alone.

Again, praying through silence is less like a microwave and more like a Crock-Pot. The longer you sit in it, the more comfortable you get when it looks like *nothing* is happening, and the more trust is grown. So rather than running from silence, what would it look like for you to welcome it? To seek it out? To stay with it and to be strengthened by it?

Imagine if Hannah hadn't stood in the face of God's silence all those years. Imagine if she had walked away. She might've never had her trust in God strengthened like it was. She might've never had her son, Samuel. Without Samuel, who would have anointed Israel's first king, Saul, and later its greatest king, David? And it is from David's kingly lineage that we have our true King, Jesus. You never know what God is growing in you in the sacred space of silence.

THE SILENCE OF JESUS

Jesus knew the value of silence. He did not run from it; he ran after it. The Gospel writers make sure that we get that silence was a part of how Jesus prayed through his journey to the Cross. Luke 5:16 says that "Jesus often withdrew to lonely places and prayed."

Lonely places. Quiet places. Places away from the noise of the world around him. Places away from the demands of the crowds. We do not know how or what Jesus prayed during these times. But we do know that he sought them out. He made time and space for quiet, for silence. And in so doing, Jesus teaches us yet again how we can pray. What if the silence of God is not something to simply endure but rather something to embrace? What if, instead of running from silence or being frustrated by it, you were able to seek it out, to claim it as a way that you pray? Can you learn not only to get comfortable with silence but also to incorporate it into your everyday life? Can you—like Hannah, like Jesus— move from resisting silence to resting in it?

Praying through silence can be challenging, but the more you practice it, the better you get at it. The less you fight it, the less you resist it, the easier it comes to you. You may not be able to start with a day or an hour, but you *can* start with five minutes. You can intentionally carve out time in the morning, before everyone else is up, or at the end of the day, after everything is done and the house is quiet. You can take your first five minutes at work, before you open your in-box. Or go for a walk during lunch. You can learn to make silence your friend so that when God *is* silent, you'll be speaking the same language. You can resist the urge to thrash about and allow yourself to rest, submerged and surrounded by God's loving presence. Allow every one of your fears, cares, concerns, and complaints to be exhaled and to float away.

When you think about it, praying through silence is perhaps one of the simplest and easiest ways for you to pray. After all, you don't have to worry about how to pray or what to say. In fact, the whole point of silence is for you to do and say nothing. Your job is just to show up. To make space. To make time. Silent prayer is not something you stumble into. It takes initiative and intentionality. Like Jesus, it requires your setting aside a time and a place away from the distractions and demands of the day. And like Hannah, it requires a commitment to keep showing up.

THE SACRED CHAIR

For me, praying through silence happens best in the morning, before the kids are up or shortly after we've dropped them off at school. It happens in our old gray chair (the first piece of "real" furniture Jeanne and I ever bought). It's usually for five minutes. Sometimes it's for ten. It consists of me setting a timer on my watch or phone—and then setting it aside, closing my eyes, breathing deeply, and sitting still. It usually takes the first couple of minutes for me to name each of my distractions and preoccupations and release them like little air bubbles. It helps me to be as specific as possible with each of these and to release them with an exhale. Then I just . . . sit. It's a conscious choice to rest in God's presence. As I find myself getting distracted and pulled back to the surface by this thought or that, I name it and release it. Sometimes I'm reminded of a verse or a truth of God. Other times, there is just silence.

I would love to tell you that this is a practice that happens every day. It is not. But it's a practice important enough to me that I have a weekly call with a friend who encourages me to seek it out. I have yet to regret making time for silence, but I can tell when I do not. I imagine those around me can as well. The more I practice it, the more comfortable I become with it, the more I desire it, and the closer I feel to God—even when he chooses to be silent.

THE OTHER SIDE OF SILENCE

There is far more than you can possibly imagine on the other side of silence. Even though it may seem like God's silence is all you know in this season, it is not all there is. I do not know why God chooses to be silent in certain seasons, but I do know that it does not last forever. Like all seasons, it gives way to another season. You may not always hear or have the answers that you seek from God, but if you are willing to stay with God through this season, you will have far more than you began with. You will no longer settle for a fair-weather faith. You will have a greater desire for the deeper things of God. You will have a peace that passes understanding; a new-found fluency in the language of silence and a camaraderie with the community of saints who have gone before you. You will know how to pray in a whole new way—on the other side of silence.

PRACTICE

This week, can you set aside three intentional times for silence? Pick a time and place where you will be the least distracted. Start with five minutes. Take the first couple of minutes to exhale every distraction and preoccupation. (This is easier said than done. You will find there is far more floating around in your soul than you imagine. That's normal.)

Take the time to name each one specifically. Trust that God will know what to do with them all. Then use the time left to rest in the reality of God's presence. That's it.

Don't worry about doing anything "right" or "wrong." Don't expect a divine revelation. Just keep showing up. Keep practicing. See if God doesn't grow your heart so you are more and more like Jesus, who sought out his heavenly Father in the still, quiet, and even lonely places.

PRAYER

Mysterious and sometimes silent God,
Here I am. Distracted by and attracted to one thousand
   different things.
Quiet my soul.
Help me to be with you here and now,
even in this silence.
Give me the heart of Hannah and the wisdom of Jesus
   to know that even though you may be silent, you
   are not absent.
Teach me to become fluent in the language of silence
and to receive from you exactly what I need and more
   than I could imagine—
your loving presence, which surrounds me even now.
Amen.

8

WHEN I AM OUT
OF WORDS

*Prayer is not what is done by us, but rather what is done
by the Holy Spirit in us.*

HENRI NOUWEN, *THE ONLY NECESSARY THING*

I've always been a talkative person—ever since I was a little
kid. My mom said that when I was little, I would talk so much
and ask so many questions that she developed a catchphrase
question to ask me when I was out of control (which was
often): "Jarrett, do you know where you're driving me?" And
without missing a beat, I would invariably answer, "Right up
da wall, Mommy!" When it came to playing the silent game
in the car, I would quit at the start, just so I could keep talking. At parent-teacher conferences, my parents would regularly hear the same feedback in various forms: "He's a good
student, but he needs to learn to let others speak." In high
school, I was drawn to and excelled in theater and speech. It

comes as a surprise to no one that as an adult, I've found a job where I get paid to talk every week.

My effectiveness as a teacher and preacher is contingent on my ability to use words. However, one Sunday a few years back, it looked like my forty-plus-year speaking streak was in real jeopardy. I had just finished the first of four services that morning at our church. While preaching at the 8:00 a.m. service, I had noticed that my throat felt dry and it was hard to swallow. By the time I finished my message and sat down, I could hardly breathe. My throat was closing, and I had no idea why . . . or how I was going to make it through the next three services! Thankfully, a nurse who is a part of our church met me and some of the team in my office. We couldn't figure out what was wrong. The next service was starting in thirty minutes, and I couldn't talk. I couldn't get a single word out. (It was a day my mom had prayed about for years. God is faithful.)

After popping some Benadryl and drinking some hot tea, my throat loosened up a little, and I pushed through the remaining three services, albeit in a more conversational tone. By the end of the day, I had no voice left. It was gone. After seeing a specialist and getting a few steroid pills, they determined that it was some sort of allergic reaction to "something." They had no idea what. Their advice to this preacher with no voice was to pray that it doesn't happen again. #Helpful.

A preacher without words is not a very effective preacher. Words are kind of an important element to the whole preaching gig. The same could be said of prayer. Words are kind of an important element to the whole praying gig. And yet there are times when you try to pray and you simply have no words to say. For whatever reason, you just don't know what to say or don't want to say anything. It may be connected to exhaustion (physical, spiritual, or emotional). It could be connected to anger toward God. It could be because of grief you are going through. Whatever the reason, odds are that at some point, you have lost your voice in prayer. Lost the ability to put a sentence together in prayer. Lost the desire to even pray. If that has ever happened to you, you are not alone. And you are not without hope. In fact, praying without words can be one of the most powerful and dynamic ways to pray. Rather than offering the advice given to me by my doctor to "pray that it doesn't happen again," I want to encourage you to pray through the moments when you have no words to say.

UNSPOKEN

One of the unique distinctions of attending Christian schools for most of my life (aside from knowing the difference between a furlong and a fathom and being able to draw a map of the Holy Land from memory) was morning prayer. Every morning, our homeroom teachers would start the day with a time of prayer. They would inevitably ask if there were any prayer requests. We would sit in awkward silence for more than a moment until someone brought up something or other about their grandma or that afternoon's soccer game. Those requests were fine and good, but another kind was what got our curiosities percolating: the silent prayer request.

Without fail, someone would raise their hand and, when called on, say the phrase that pays: "I have a silent prayer request." The silent prayer request was the Uno Wild Card of prayer. It could mean *anything*! We had another name for these redacted requests. We called them "Unspokens." The Unspoken Prayer Request was a way of getting people to pray for you without telling them what to pray for. We knew that God knew what this unspoken request was about, but that didn't stop us from having our own prayer conspiracy theories. In our heads, we would try to crack the case of the silent prayer request. Like little prayer mentalists, we would run down a list of options:

> *Brad asked for an Unspoken prayer. I wonder what it's about. I did see him and his girlfriend fighting yesterday—I bet it's that. Or maybe his parents are fighting, and he doesn't want us to know. Or maybe his family is in the witness-protection program, and the mob finally caught up to them. Is Brad even his real name?*

At the time, the silent (aka Unspoken) prayer request felt like a prayer cop-out to me. My thought was, *If you want to pray for something or you want someone to pray for you, say it. Be specific. Use words. Don't make God (or more specifically, me) guess!*

But the longer I have lived this life of prayer, the more I've come to experience and appreciate prayer without words. I have discovered what countless generations before us have been trying to teach us: There are other ways to say what my heart needs to say without having to use words. Without having to use words *at all.* And that when you find yourself speechless before God, for whatever reason, it does not mean that something is wrong with you or broken. It means that God is inviting you into something new, a way of praying through whatever you are facing—even when you don't have words.

SIRI . . . OUSLY?

We live in the age of the digital assistant. When Jeanne and I were dating (pre–dial-up Internet), if I wanted to take her to a nice restaurant for dinner, I had to look up the number in the phone book (we used to print the Internet), call the restaurant (when they were open), talk to a person, and make a reservation. Now, Siri can do it all for me (the reservation part, not the date itself). Digital assistants like Siri and Alexa not only make reservations for us but also provide navigation, order groceries, and schedule appointments. I heard a story recently of a man who had a falling out with his regular barber and couldn't figure out why. When he dug deeper, he found out that thanks to a new beta feature, his Google Assistant had called and made multiple haircut appointments that the man didn't know about. It called the place where he got his hair cut and, in an approximated human voice, had a conversation with an actual human being to set up an appointment— multiple times! This is how the robot wars begin.

We have become increasingly more comfortable with digital assistants handling our menial tasks, but we have yet to entrust our most important jobs to them. You wouldn't ask Alexa to apologize to your wife for forgetting your anniversary, or have Siri tell someone at work that they're fired. Thankfully, we haven't crossed that ethical bridge . . . yet.

When it comes to prayer—specifically, when you have no words to pray—the good news is that God has already given you an assistant: One who is intimately connected to you and to God. One who can speak to God on your behalf with words that you alone cannot utter. One who can help your defeated or depleted heart hear from God. The Holy Spirit is your way to pray when you don't have words to say.

YOUR SPIRITUAL ASSISTANT

In Romans 8, Paul lets you know that God is not only already *with* you in prayer but also *for* you. The Holy Spirit works on your behalf even when nothing seems to be working in prayer.

> We do not know what we ought to pray for, but the Spirit himself intercedes for us through wordless groans.
> ROMANS 8:26

This is a paradigm shift. You are never alone in prayer. Even when you don't know what to say or don't want to say anything, the Holy Spirit *in* you is praying *for* you *with* God. This means that your prayers aren't merely going *up* to God (as we explored earlier) but are also coming *through* the Holy Spirit. The Holy Spirit gives you the words to

say—even when you don't know what to say. The Holy
Spirit says it all for you in a way that goes beyond words.
God is already with you, helping you pray! The Spirit
turns your groans into glory, your struggle into something
spiritual!

Paul goes on, saying,

> He who searches our hearts knows the mind of the
> Spirit, because the Spirit intercedes for God's people
> in accordance with the will of God.
> ROMANS 8:27

In the same way that there is perfect connection and oneness within the Trinity, the Holy Spirit has a connection and
oneness with you and me that we are largely unaware of. The
Spirit within you knows you better than you know yourself.

The Spirit knows how to say
what you don't know how to or are
unwilling to say. The Holy Spirit is
your translator and your transistor!
The Spirit is both the *way* you pray
and the *words* you pray! The Spirit
always prays in alignment with
God's perfect will—even when you don't know what God's
will is. When you're praying for something that isn't God's
will, the Spirit leads you to God's will—if you are willing to
open yourself up. That is such a gift from God!

But it is important to note that while the Holy Spirit is

**The Holy Spirit gives you
the words to pray—even
when you don't know
what to say.**

there to help you in your weakness, he is not there to help you in your absence. You have to do your part. You have to show up—even if you have nothing to say.

JESUS, TAKE THE WHEEL

A few years back, I had my first experience "driving" a Tesla. I say "driving" because I barely did. My friend Jeff has a Tesla with the upgraded autopilot feature, which means that once you turn it on, the car takes over. It maintains your speed and distance from other cars perfectly. Use the turn signal, and it waits for the perfect moment for you to change lanes—and then does it for you. It's a disorienting and delightful experience. It's truly hands-free driving (which, if I'm being honest, I've been doing for years. The old "drive with your knees while eating a meatball sub" was a move I pulled off more than a few times in college).

> The Spirit will pray for you—but simply will not pray without you.

One of the smartest aspects that Tesla designed into its autopilot feature is the need to put your hands back on the steering wheel every few minutes. A beeper goes off in the car as if to ask, "Are you still there? Are you still awake? Are you still checking Instagram?" Once you put your hands back on the steering wheel for a few seconds, the autopilot continues. In other words, while the Tesla can drive without you steering, it cannot drive without you. At least not at the time I'm writing this. You still have to be in the car. It can assist you, but it cannot drive without you.

And that's the way the Holy Spirit works when you show up in prayer. The Holy Spirit is your partner in prayer to guide, guard, and lead you into alignment with God's will. The Spirit will continue to do this until God's will becomes the thing you pray for most in your life. The Spirit will be your words when there are no words to say. The Spirit will pray for you—but simply will not pray without you.

So how can you still pray when there aren't words to say? Thankfully, there are ways to pray beyond words. There are practical prayer practices that you can learn from and lean on when words won't come.

MOVE YOUR BODY

God has given you a way to pray when you find yourself wanting to pray but wanting for words. It's a way that has been with you your entire life, since before you even learned to pray or speak: your body. Your body is one of the most powerful ways you can pray. You can say so much to God without even saying a word.

Think about all the ways that you already use your body for nonverbal communication. When you see someone you love and maybe haven't seen for a while and open your arms to them, what are you saying? You're saying that you love them, you welcome them, and you're available to them. If you have children and bust them for eating industrial-strength snow-melting salt off the driveway after being told not to (true

> You can say so much to God without even saying a word.

story), and they hang their heads low, what are they saying? That they're sorry. That they feel guilt. And that most likely, they are about to throw up after eating road salt. Our bodies can say what sometimes our words cannot.

Whether it's Professor Albert Mehrabian's initial (albeit not completely accurate) discovery that 55 percent of communication is nonverbal[1] or the more recent and robust University of Pennsylvania study that concluded that 70 percent of communication is through body language,[2] the point is that we say a lot to one another with our bodies. So why wouldn't the same be true of how we communicate with God?

Hands-Open Prayer

If you happened to grow up in or around church, then you were most likely taught to pray with your eyes closed and your hands folded. That's how I was taught to pray. There's not a Bible verse that says to do that. It's just what you were taught. My theory is it's meant to keep kids from getting distracted or poking the people next to them while praying. There's nothing wrong with that, but what is your body saying with your eyes closed and hands folded? I think there's a better way to use your body in prayer. That's why years ago at Soul City Church, we began the practice of praying with our hands open. We think that our hands say so much more when we do. Having your hands open in prayer says, *My hands are open, my heart is open, and my life is open to whatever it is that you have for me and ask of me, God.* By sitting in silence with your hands open, you can communicate your openness, willingness, and availability to God. Recently, our kids had some church friends over to hang out at our house. When we gathered for dinner and it was time to pray, I noticed each of them opening their hands as Gigi thanked God for our meal (which was deep-dish pizza, so we knew it had already been blessed by God).

Kneeling Prayer

Another prayer posture that you can practice is kneeling. Maybe you are in a church with kneelers built into the pews, like some sort of reverse La-Z-Boy recliner. Maybe over time kneeling became more about tradition than transformation. But I believe it's a powerful way you can use to communicate to God that you trust and submit to his will and ways. It's a posture of humility: When you kneel, your body says that there is a God and that you are not him. Just two minutes of silent kneeling can say so much more than your mouth might ever be able to say.

Hands-On Prayer

Placing a hand over part of your body that represents a place where you need healing (either physically or metaphorically), help, or forgiveness is another way you can use your body to pray. If you find yourself overwhelmed with anxious thoughts or distracted by a thousand things, simply place your hand on your head and sit in silence. If your eyes keep you from seeing the ways God is lovingly moving in your life, place your hand over your eyes. If your words keep getting you into trouble, cover your mouth. If your heart is broken or hurting . . . you get the point. Place your hand where you most need God in your body or your life, and the Holy Spirit will do the rest. You don't even have to say a thing.

Standing Prayer

Another powerful prayer posture is simply standing. Unlike sitting or kneeling, standing before God is a way to declare your right to be in his presence—and to remind yourself that you are. It's a way to claim access to standing before the very throne of God, which Jesus made possible. If you have a hard time believing that God loves you or even likes you, try standing upright in prayer. Maybe even tilt your head up, as if toward heaven. Standing is a way to claim what Jesus says is yours and remind yourself that you are his beloved child. God calls you his own, and you can stand on the authority of that identity.

Eyes-Wide-Open Prayer

I offer this last prayer posture with a slight word of warning. My friend Eric calls it "Freestyle Prayer." Years ago, when Eric was an intern at our church, he initiated his own prayer posture. He was in a particularly difficult season with God: He wasn't sure where his life was going, and he wasn't particularly interested in praying. When Jeanne and I would gather with interns and pray, everyone would close their eyes—everyone except Eric. During these prayer times, he would sit there with his eyes wide open. Every now and then I would quickly open my eyes, only to find Eric staring right at all of us in the circle. It had the equivalent effect of seeing someone standing outside your window. It was jarring, to say the least. And once I sneaked a peek at Eric with his eyes opened in prayer, I couldn't help but check to see if they were still open a couple of minutes later (they were). Eventually I asked him about it, and he told me that it was an intentional (albeit slightly creepy) way of breaking from unconscious habits and prayer patterns that meant and offered little to him in that season. It was a way for him to be present in prayer. So if you find prayer rote and stale, give "Eyes-Wide-Open Prayer" a try. But maybe give everyone else a heads-up first.

My friend and mentor Jim says that "the body never lies." Your body simply does not know how to lie. It only knows how to represent what is, which is why taking a posture of prayer may be one of the most important things you can do to represent what is most true to God. Take what you already use in so much of how you communicate with others and begin communicating with God in the same way. You may find that even though you don't have words, you have so much more to say.

PRAYERFUL PLAGIARISM

I was taught in school that plagiarism is a bad thing, that claiming someone else's work as your own is unacceptable, even unforgivable. As a young preacher and communicator, I was taught to never poach someone else's sermon. I watched pastors and authors lose credibility while facing charges of plagiarism. But in the copy-and-paste world we live in, it's almost impossible to even know whose work is whose anymore.

I still believe that plagiarism is a bad thing in writing or speaking, but I've come to find it a gift in prayer. A few years back, I hit a wall. I had been going nonstop for five years, getting Soul City Church off the ground. I was finishing a book (or at least trying to). I had been preaching every Sunday for more than forty weeks per year for years. I had been doing so much *for* God that my intentional time *with* God was suffering, to say the least. The only prayer I knew how to pray was "God, I'm so tired." It was in this season that I discovered the art of prayerful plagiarism. My friend Ruth Haley Barton introduced me to a little book by Ted Loder called *Guerrillas of Grace*. I had never heard of him or this book, but it became a lifeline to me. The book was written decades ago and is filled with the most beautiful and gut-wrenchingly honest prayers. They became my prayers.

Here is a section of one of those prayers that I prayed (and still pray):

O God,
let something essential happen to me,
   something more than interesting
      or entertaining,
         or thoughtful.
O God,
let something essential happen to me,
   something awesome,
      something real.
Speak to my condition, Lord,
and change me somewhere inside where it matters,
a change that will burn and tremble and heal
   and explode me into tears
      or laughter
         or love that throbs or screams
            or keeps a terrible, cleansing silence
               and dares the dangerous deeds.
Let something happen in me
which is my real self, God.[3]

Leaning on the words that others have spoken to God when you have no words of your own is one of the most helpful and valuable things you can do. You can own words that are not your own. Why do you think God included the book of Psalms in the Bible? It takes up significant prime-location real estate, and it's exclusively others' prayers. No history, no teachings, no genealogies—just prayers. It contains the words of others who came before you who wrestled and wrangled with God. Who danced and delighted in God. Who called out and cried out to God. These words are there for the taking, for you to pray when you don't have words to say. To lean on. To learn from. To borrow. To plagiarize. To make your own. Rather than reading or reciting them, what if you could embody them and make them your words to God?

LEANING ON OTHERS

Another way you can pray when you don't have words to say is by leaning on others' prayers. I hesitate to even offer this because it seems so obvious, but I wonder what it would look like for you to honestly and earnestly ask others to pray for you—not in a silent prayer request sort of way, but in a more deliberately desperate way. Who in your life can you go to and say, "I don't know what to pray. I don't have words to pray. Will you pray *for* me?"? And when I say "for," I don't mean, "Hey, if you happen to get to it." No. I mean, "Right here. Right now. Will you be my words? Will you be my advocate? Will you do with me and for me what I can't seem to do on my own?" Be specific. Be honest. Be vulnerable. Be bold. Can you have the courage to borrow some of their faith in this season and even in this moment? My hunch is that you will find folks who are more than willing to stand in that spiritual gap with and for you, who will make *their* words *your* words—people who will tangibly and audibly do for you what the Holy Spirit is already doing for you.

WITHOUT WORDS

My wife Jeanne and I have been in love for more than twenty-five years. That's a long time. We've shared a lot of words. Our first words came while we dated long-distance. They were through handwritten letters and landline phone calls that went late into the night. We've used a lot of words in our time together. We have yet to run out of things to say to each other, and I doubt we ever will. And

> **Prayer is essential for your relationship with God. Words are not.**

yet there are times that we don't need words, times when we can just sit together while reading, hold hands while walking, or hold each other at night. We can say more to each other in these sacred moments than we can in a thousand words.

Prayer is essential for your relationship with God. Words are not. God knows your heart even when you don't know what to say. And he's promised you the presence of his Holy Spirit, your prayer advocate and ally—the one who speaks to God for you when words cannot be found or are not enough. He's given you your body as a way to pray, to physically inhabit your prayers through postures and gestures. He's given you the prayers of others, prayers that you can hitch your heart to when words are wanting. And he's given you others who can stand with and for you before God, others who would love to lend their faith for the season you find yourself in.

You are unique in so many ways. There is no one else like you. But you are not the first person to run out of words in prayer. And if you find yourself in that season even now, it probably won't be the last time. Thankfully God has already given you all you need to wade through this wordless season. And in time, the words will come. Not at first, but I promise you—they will. They will be drawn from a deeper well. They will matter more. And you will be a better person for having walked through this season. You can take my word for it.

PRACTICE

I want to invite you into a subtle spiritual shift. When you come to pray, open your hands. Whether words flow or you sit in silence, open your hands. If you go to church and someone prays, open your hands. When you're stressed out at work, take sixty seconds of silence to place your open hands on your desk. Practice opening your hands to God every time you think to pray. This simple prayer posture says so much to you and to God. It's your way of being present and open to him; of welcoming what he offers and offering what you have; of being both expectant and available—whether words come or not.

PRAYER

(Sit silently with your hands open to God for sixty seconds.)

Amen.

CONCLUSION

AMEN

"Amen" is not the end of a prayer;
it just gets us ready to go to the next level.

AMERICAN TREASURE GARY BUSEY

As I said in the beginning of this book, you already know how to pray. No matter how hard or challenging it may seem, no matter how new you are to it or how long you've been at it, you are already awesome at praying. Just by showing up in prayer, you are further than you may even realize. By showing up in your joy and gratitude, in your fear and worry, in your grief and silence, you are saying that there is more. There is more than this moment. There is more than this season. There is more—and God is enough. By showing up in prayer, however you get there, you are saying that you believe that God is here, that he hears, and that he has what you most need.

Prayer is a radical reorienting of your everyday world. It is your way of seeing through and beyond what is right in front of you. It is your profession and confession that there is a God and that you need him more than you know. It is your way of being in constant connection with God. Gone are the days of go-betweens (priest and prophets, the Temple and the Tabernacle). There is nothing that stands between you and the God of the universe. And the crazy thing is that he is already waiting for you in prayer. You don't have to try to get his attention. You don't have to try to earn his ear—it's already yours, if you only pray.

Having grown up around praying people most of my life, I have met those who some might consider prayer masters: People who pray for hours on end. People who have been praying year after year. People who can pray the roof off. And people who can sit in silence and solitude. And while they may seem like prayer pros, the truth is that no one is a master at prayer, because prayer is not meant to be mastered. It cannot be mastered any more than love can be mastered. No one figures out love. It only draws us in deeper and deeper, opening up our hearts more and more. The same is true of prayer.

I have found that praying through is my way through.

The more you show up in prayer, the more you grow up in prayer. The more you show up as you are, whatever feeling you may be feeling, whatever season you may be going through, the more you grow in prayer. Prayer has no end.

Even though we may add a word like *Amen* to the end of it, there is no end to prayer. But that doesn't mean that it won't get easier. That doesn't mean that it won't become more natural to you. Like all things that you now know how to do, it takes time, practice, and humility. It takes a willingness to show up, to make it more than an accessory to your life—to make it a necessity until it becomes a thing you can't imagine living without.

I have found that praying through is my way through. It is my way through this life. It is my lifeline. It is my anchor. It is my constant. It is not how I escape whatever I am going through; it is how I face whatever I am going through.

And that is my prayer for you. I pray that prayer becomes *your* way no matter how clumsy or poetic you are or whether words flow or cease. That in every high and every low, you know you have a way through, that you have a God who knows you, loves you, and is waiting for you in prayer. And that you would grow in prayer and *because* of prayer. That you would stumble across this book years from now and not be the same person. That through whatever season may come, you will always know that you can always pray. That you can come to God as you are and, through prayer, become who he created you to be.

Amen.

THANKS TO . . .

I am beyond thankful for my family. Jeanne, Elijah, and Gigi, your loving prayer and support for this book are what kept me going and believing that God had actually given me something to say. Thank you for being my home base. You are the place that I go out from and come home to.

Thank you, Soul City Church, for being the reason that I write. You are a remarkable and inspiring group of people. You are my people. And Jeanne and I are proud to be your pastors.

Thank you to my NavPress team: Don, Zim, Elizabeth, Jen Phelps, and the rest of the NavPress family. Thank you for how faithfully and diligently you worked and prayed for me as I worked on this book about prayer. Simply put, you helped to make me a better writer and this book the best that it can be.

Thank you to my old friend and agent, Angela Scheff of the Christopher Ferebee Agency. From editing my first book fifteen years ago to your wisdom and advice along the way to helping to bring this book into the world, I am so very grateful for you, Angela.

And lastly, I want to honor and thank my spiritual directors and mentors throughout the years. To Sibyl Towner, Sheryl Fleischer, Ruth Haley Barton, Jim Dethmer, and Fr. Richard Rohr: Thank you. Your words, presence, partnership, and direction over the years reverberate throughout my life and come through on these pages. You have lovingly and faithfully invited me into the deeper places with God. You taught me, walked with me, prayed with me, and prayed me through just about every season I write about in this book. For that, I am eternally grateful.

NOTES

FOREWORD
1. Luke 11:1.
2. Thomas Merton, *Contemplative Prayer* (New York: Image Books, 1996), 13.
3. Dallas Willard, *The Divine Conspiracy: Rediscovering Our Hidden Life in God* (New York: HarperOne, 1997), 232.

INTRODUCTION
1. Martyn Lloyd-Jones, *The Assurance of Our Salvation: Exploring the Depth of Jesus' Prayer for His Own*, Studies in John 17 (Wheaton, IL: Crossway, 2000), chap. 2.
2. D. Martyn Lloyd-Jones, *Studies in the Sermon on the Mount*, one-vol. ed. (Grand Rapids, MI: Eerdmans, 1976), 322.

1—WHEN EVERYTHING IS NEW
1. Andrew Murray, *Humility: The Journey toward Holiness* (Minneapolis: Bethany House, 2001), 107.
2. This phrase is not included in all translations of the Bible. Some scholars believe it to be inspired (and therefore think it should be included) while others do not.
3. Anne Lamott, *Help, Thanks, Wow: The Three Essential Prayers* (New York: Riverhead Books, 2012).
4. These names of God are used throughout the Bible and throughout Christian history. They remind us of the character and ability of God. *Jehovah Jireh*: The Lord Will Provide; *Jehovah Nissi*: The Lord Is My Banner; *Jehovah Rapha*: The Lord Who Heals (or Restores); *Jehovah Roi*: The Lord Who Sees Me.

2—WHEN I NEED TO SAY THANKS

1. Eric Mosley and Derek Irvine, *The Power of Thanks: How Social Recognition Empowers Employees and Creates a Best Place to Work* (New York: McGraw-Hill Education, 2014), 31–32.
2. Mosley and Irvine, *Power of Thanks*, 33.
3. Originally published in Yiddish as *Un di velt hot geshvign* (*And the World Has Remained Silent*). Wiesel was eventually awarded a Nobel Peace Prize for his "universal condemnation of all violence, hatred, and oppression" expressed through writing and lectures. *Encyclopaedia Britannica*, s.v. "Elie Wiesel," accessed May 31, 2019, https://www.britannica.com/biography/Elie-Wiesel. See also "The Nobel Peace Prize for 1986," nobelprize.org, accessed May 31, 2019, https://www.nobelprize.org/prizes/peace/1986/press-release/.
4. "Oprah Talks to Elie Wiesel," Oprah.com, accessed June 3, 2019, https://www.oprah.com/omagazine/Oprah-Interviews-Elie-Wiesel/2.
5. "Oprah Talks to Elie Wiesel."
6. "FDR Establishes Modern Thanksgiving Holiday," History, updated July 28, 2019, https://www.history.com/this-day-in-history/fdr-establishes-modern-thanksgiving-holiday.
7. "Proclamation of Thanksgiving," Abraham Lincoln Online, accessed June 4, 2019, http://www.abrahamlincolnonline.org/lincoln/speeches/thanks.htm.
8. Although I do not consider myself a hiker, I have several friends who are. They are the ones who told me about this small and vital tool that can be used in cases of emergency when water is in short supply. See Tim MacWelch, "Survival Skills: How to Get Water and Syrup from Trees," *Outdoor Life* (blog), February 11, 2013, https://www.outdoorlife.com/blogs/survivalist/2013/02/survival-skills-how-get-water-and-syrup-trees.

3—WHEN I NEED HELP

1. The fact that Chicago has a history of shady politics is no secret. But the details and specifics of how far and for how long politicians were/are willing to bend and break the rules of politics is a fascinating read. For more, see Mary Frances Berry, "Election Fraud Chicago Style: Illinois' Decades-Old Notoriety for Election Corruption Is Legendary," Salon, February 14, 2016, https://www.salon.com/2016/02/14/election_fraud_chicago_style_illinois_decades_old_notoriety_for_election_corruption_is_legendary/.
2. The history of this phrase is obscure. See Barbara Lerman-Golomb, "Vote Early, Vote Often (Just Not in the Same Election)," *HuffPost*,

November 7, 2016, https://www.huffpost.com/entry/vote-early-vote
-often_b_12842358.

3. "Portillo's Famous Chocolate Cake," Portillo's, accessed June 7, 2019,
   https://www.portillos.com/portillo-sfamous-chocolate-cake/.

4—WHEN I AM WORRIED

1. Ken Weliever, "Why Worry When You Can Pray," The Preachers Word,
   May 9, 2017, https://thepreachersword.com/2017/05/09/why-worry
   -when-you-can-pray/#more-10644.
2. "How Worrying Affects the Body," WebMD, accessed June 25, 2019,
   https://www.webmd.com/balance/guide/how-worrying-affects-your
   -body#1.
3. Lloyd-Jones, *Studies in the Sermon on the Mount*, 417.
4. "How Much Time Do You Spend Worrying?," IOL, August 24, 2015,
   https://www.iol.co.za/entertainment/celebrity-news/how-much-time
   -do-you-spend-worrying-1904679.

5—WHEN I AM GRIPPED BY GRIEF

1. C. S. Lewis, *A Grief Observed* (New York: HarperOne, 1994), 56.
2. Henry Cloud (@DrHenryCloud), Facebook, January 8, 2018, https://
   www.facebook.com/DrHenryCloud/posts/grief-is-accepting-the-reality
   -of-what-is-that-is-griefs-job-and-purpose-to-allo/10156072817589571/.
3. Jerry Sittser, *A Grace Disguised: How the Soul Grows through Loss*
   (Grand Rapids, MI: Zondervan, 2004), 49.

6—WHEN I NEED DIRECTION

1. Quoted in Larry Chang, comp. and ed., *Wisdom for the Soul: Five
   Millennia of Prescriptions for Spiritual Healing* (Washington, DC:
   Gnosophia, 2006), 457.
2. Dietrich Bonhoeffer, *Letters and Papers from Prison*, abr. (London: SCM
   Press, 2017), 137.

7—WHEN I DON'T HEAR ANYTHING

1. Andrew Peterson, "The Silence of God," *Love and Thunder* copyright ©
   2003 Essential Records.

8—WHEN I AM OUT OF WORDS

1. Nagesh Belludi, "Albert Mehrabian's 7–38–55 Rule of Personal
   Communication," Right Attitudes: Ideas for Impact, October 4, 2008,
   https://www.rightattitudes.com/2008/10/04/7-38-55-rule-personal
   -communication/.

2. Aurora Employee Assistance Program, "The Art of Communication," accessed June 25, 2019, https://www.marquette.edu/hr/documents/the-art-of-communication.pdf.

3. Ted Loder, *Guerrilla of Grace: Prayers for the Battle* (Minneapolis: Augsburg Fortress, 1981), 92.

ABOUT THE AUTHOR

Jarrett Stevens is a pastor, writer, and public speaker. His several books include *Four Small Words: A Simple Way to Understand the Bible* and *The Deity Formerly Known as God*. Known for his humor and honesty, Jarrett is a popular speaker at churches and conferences, both nationally and internationally. He lives with his family in downtown Chicago, where he and his wife, Jeanne, pastor the church they planted, Soul City.

TWITTER: @jarrettstevens
INSTAGRAM: jarrettstevens

THE NAVIGATORS® STORY

———— ◉ ————

T HANK YOU for picking up this NavPress book! I hope it has been a blessing to you.

NavPress is a ministry of The Navigators. The Navigators began in the 1930s, when a young California lumberyard worker named Dawson Trotman was impacted by basic discipleship principles and felt called to teach those principles to others. He saw this mission as an echo of 2 Timothy 2:2: "And the things you have heard me say in the presence of many witnesses entrust to reliable people who will also be qualified to teach others" (NIV).

In 1933, Trotman and his friends began discipling members of the US Navy. By the end of World War II, thousands of men on ships and bases around the world were learning the principles of spiritual multiplication by the intentional, person-to-person teaching of God's Word.

After World War II, The Navigators expanded its relational ministry to include college campuses; local churches; the Glen Eyrie Conference Center and Eagle Lake Camps in Colorado Springs, Colorado; and neighborhood and citywide initiatives across the country and around the world.

Today, with more than 2,600 US staff members—and local ministries in more than 100 countries—The Navigators continues the transformational process of making disciples who make more disciples, advancing the Kingdom of God in a world that desperately needs the hope and salvation of Jesus Christ and the encouragement to grow deeper in relationship with Him.

NAVPRESS was created in 1975 to advance the calling of The Navigators by bringing biblically rooted and culturally relevant products to people who want to know and love Christ more deeply. In January 2014, NavPress entered an alliance with Tyndale House Publishers to strengthen and better position our rich content for the future. Through *THE MESSAGE* Bible and other resources, NavPress seeks to bring positive spiritual movement to people's lives.

If you're interested in learning more or becoming involved with The Navigators, go to www.navigators.org. For more discipleship content from The Navigators and NavPress authors, visit www.thedisciplemaker.org. May God bless you in your walk with Him!

Sincerely,

DON PAPE
VP/PUBLISHER, NAVPRESS

www.navpress.com

CP1308